NUTRACEUTICALS

OCCURRENCE, BENEFITS, AND REGULATIONS

DR. MURALIDHAR RAO AKKALADEVI

Made with ♥ on the Notion Press Platform
www.notionpress.com

Contents

Contents

Preface

Nutraceuticals have gained immense popularity in recent years due to their potential health benefits and disease prevention properties. Nutraceuticals are bioactive compounds that are found in foods and have been shown to improve human health and well-being. The demand for nutraceutical products is increasing globally, and it has become essential to have a comprehensive understanding of the science behind these compounds.

This book on "Nutraceuticals: Occurrence, Benefits, and Regulations" is a compilation of research on various nutraceutical compounds, their chemical nature, and their medicinal benefits. It provides a comprehensive overview of the current state of knowledge on phytochemicals, free radicals, and food laws and regulations related to nutraceuticals.

The book is divided into five units, covering topics such as the classification of nutraceuticals, health problems and diseases that can be prevented or cured by nutraceuticals, and the occurrence and characteristic features of various phytochemicals such as carotenoids, sulfides, polyphenolics, flavonoids, prebiotics, probiotics, and tocopherols.

The book also discusses the role of free radicals in various diseases such as diabetes, inflammation, cancer, atherosclerosis, and ageing, as well as the importance of antioxidants in protecting against free radical damage. Additionally, it covers food laws and regulations related to nutraceuticals, including FDA, FPO, MPO, AGMARK, HACCP, and GMPs.

This book is intended to serve as a valuable resource for students, researchers, healthcare professionals, and anyone interested in understanding the science behind nutraceuticals and their potential role in disease prevention and management. We hope that this book will contribute to the growing body of knowledge on nutraceuticals and promote further research in this field.

Dr.Muralidhar Rao akkaladevi

13-03-2023

NUTRACEUTICALS

Occurrence, Benefits, and Regulations

Dr.Muralidhar Rao Akkaladevi

Publisher
Notion Press
Notion Press, Inc.
800, West EI Camino Real #180,
California USA 94040
Notion Press Media Pvt Ltd,
#7, Red Cross Road,
Egmore, Chennai, Tamil Nadu 600008
Email ID: publish@notionpress.com
Phone Number: +91 44 46315631

I

Functional Foods, Nutraceuticals, and Dietary Supplements: Sources and Health Benefits

I. Introduction

A. Definition of Nutraceuticals, Functional Foods, and Dietary Supplements

Nutraceuticals are bioactive compounds that are derived from food sources and have potential health benefits beyond basic nutritional functions. They can be extracted from various parts of plants, animals, and microorganisms and can be consumed as supplements or as part of a balanced diet.

Functional foods, on the other hand, are whole foods or fortified foods that provide health benefits beyond basic nutritional functions. They contain one or more bioactive compounds that may reduce the risk of chronic diseases when consumed regularly.

Dietary supplements are products that are intended to supplement the diet and contain one or more dietary ingredients such as vitamins, minerals, herbs, or other botanicals, amino acids, and other substances. They are available in various forms such as tablets, capsules, powders, and liquids.

B. Importance of Nutraceuticals in Disease Prevention and Management

1. Nutraceuticals have received significant attention in recent years due to their potential role in disease prevention and management.
   Cardiovascular disease is a leading cause of death worldwide, and nutraceuticals such as garlic, ginseng, and soybean have been found to have beneficial effects on blood pressure, cholesterol levels, and overall cardiovascular health. These compounds can help reduce inflammation, improve endothelial function, and regulate lipid metabolism, which are all key factors in preventing cardiovascular disease.

   Diabetes is another major health concern that affects millions of people worldwide. Nutraceuticals such as spirulina and flaxseeds have been found to have potential benefits in managing blood sugar levels and reducing insulin resistance. These compounds contain bioactive components such as phycocyanin and lignans, which have been shown to improve glucose metabolism and insulin sensitivity.

Obesity is a major risk factor for several chronic diseases, including cardiovascular disease and diabetes. Nutraceuticals such as broccoli and ginseng have been found to have potential benefits in weight management. These compounds contain bioactive components such as sulforaphane and ginsenosides, which can help regulate appetite, boost metabolism, and reduce inflammation.

Cancer is a complex disease that can be caused by various factors, including genetic mutations, environmental factors, and lifestyle choices. Nutraceuticals such as garlic and ginkgo have been found to have potential anti-cancer effects. These compounds contain bioactive components such as allicin and flavonoids, which have been shown to have antioxidant, anti-inflammatory, and anti-tumor properties.

Overall, nutraceuticals have the potential to play a significant role in preventing and managing chronic diseases. However, it is important to note that nutraceuticals should not be used as a replacement for medical treatment or as a substitute for a healthy diet and lifestyle. It is also essential to consult with a healthcare professional before using any nutraceuticals, as they may interact with medications or have adverse effects in certain individuals.

2. Nutraceuticals have been shown to possess various biological activities such as antioxidant, anti-inflammatory, and anti-cancer properties, which make them attractive for disease prevention and

management. They may also provide additional benefits such as improved cognitive function, immune system function, and gastrointestinal health.

For example, Spirulina, a type of blue-green algae, is rich in nutrients such as protein, vitamins, and minerals, and has been shown to have antioxidant and anti-inflammatory properties. It may also have potential benefits in managing conditions such as diabetes, high cholesterol, and liver damage.

Soybean is another nutraceutical that has gained attention for its potential health benefits. Soy contains isoflavones, which are phytoestrogens that have been associated with reduced risk of certain types of cancer and improved cardiovascular health. It may also have potential benefits in managing conditions such as osteoporosis and menopausal symptoms.

Ginseng is a traditional medicinal herb that has been used for thousands of years in traditional Chinese medicine. It has been shown to have various health benefits, including anti-inflammatory and anti-cancer properties, improved cognitive function, and reduced fatigue.

Garlic is a common culinary herb that has also been used for medicinal purposes for centuries. It contains compounds such as allicin and sulfur, which have been shown to have anti-inflammatory and anti-cancer properties. Garlic may also have potential benefits in managing conditions such as high blood pressure and high cholesterol.

Broccoli is a cruciferous vegetable that is rich in nutrients such as fiber, vitamins, and minerals. It also contains compounds such as sulforaphane, which has been shown to have anti-cancer properties. Broccoli may also have potential benefits in managing conditions such as inflammation and oxidative stress.

Gingko is a tree species that has been used in traditional medicine for thousands of years. It contains flavonoids and terpenoids, which have been shown to have antioxidant and anti-inflammatory properties. Gingko may also have potential benefits in improving cognitive function and reducing symptoms of anxiety and depression.

Flaxseeds are a rich source of fiber, omega-3 fatty acids, and lignans, which have been associated with reduced risk of certain types of cancer and improved cardiovascular health. Flaxseeds may also have potential benefits in managing conditions such as diabetes and inflammation.

3. Nutraceuticals are generally considered safe and have fewer side effects compared to pharmaceutical drugs, which makes them a desirable alternative for those who are seeking natural and non-invasive approaches to improve their health.However, it is important to note that nutraceuticals, like any other supplement or medication, can interact with other drugs and may have adverse effects in certain individuals. It is recommended to consult with a healthcare professional before starting any nutraceutical regimen, especially if one is already taking other medications. Additionally, it is important to ensure the quality and purity of the nutraceutical products, as there have been reports of adulteration and contamination in the supplement industry.

II. Classification of Nutraceuticals Classification based on source and bioactive

compounds

Nutraceuticals can be classified based on their source and the bioactive compounds they contain. The following are some of the commonly used classifications of nutraceuticals:

Plant-based nutraceuticals: These are derived from plants and include phytochemicals such as carotenoids, flavonoids, and phenolic acids.

Animal-based nutraceuticals: These are derived from animals and include substances such as chondroitin, glucosamine, and omega-3 fatty acids.

Microbial-based nutraceuticals: These are derived from microorganisms such as bacteria and include probiotics and prebiotics.

Nutraceuticals based on bioactive compounds: This classification is based on the bioactive compounds present in the nutraceuticals. For example, some nutraceuticals may contain antioxidants such as vitamin C and E, while others may contain anti-inflammatory compounds such as omega-3 fatty acids.

III. Health problems and diseases that can be prevented or managed by Nutraceuticals

Nutraceuticals have been found to be effective in the prevention and management of various health problems and diseases. Some of the diseases that can be prevented or managed using nutraceuticals are:

Weight control: Nutraceuticals such as green tea extract, conjugated linoleic acid, and chitosan have been found to be effective in weight management.

Diabetes: Nutraceuticals such as chromium, alpha-lipoic acid, and cinnamon have been found to be effective in managing diabetes.

Cancer: Nutraceuticals such as curcumin, resveratrol, and green tea extract have been found to have anti-cancer properties.

Cardiovascular diseases: Nutraceuticals such as omega-3 fatty acids, CoQ10, and garlic have been found to be effective in managing cardiovascular diseases.

Cognitive function: Nutraceuticals such as omega-3 fatty acids, ginkgo biloba, and phosphatidylserine have been found to improve cognitive function.

III. Examples of nutraceuticals from plants, animals, and microorganisms

Plants:

Spirulina - a blue-green alga that contains high levels of protein, vitamins, minerals, and antioxidants. It is commonly used as a nutritional supplement and has been shown to have potential health benefits, including lowering blood pressure and improving lipid levels.

Soybean - a legume that is rich in protein, fiber, and a range of bioactive compounds such as isoflavones and phytosterols. Soybeans and their products have been studied extensively for their potential health benefits, including reducing the risk of heart disease, osteoporosis, and some forms of cancer.

Garlic - a member of the allium family that is rich in sulfur-containing compounds such as allicin, which has been shown to have potent antioxidant and anti-inflammatory properties. Garlic has been used for centuries in traditional medicine and is thought to have a range of health benefits, including reducing the risk of cardiovascular disease and certain types of cancer.

Broccoli - a cruciferous vegetable that is high in fiber, vitamins, minerals, and a range of phytochemicals such as sulforaphane and glucosinolates. Broccoli and other cruciferous vegetables have been shown to have potential health benefits, including reducing the risk of cancer, heart disease, and cognitive decline.

Ginkgo - a tree native to China that contains a range of bioactive compounds such as flavonoids and terpenoids. Ginkgo has been used in traditional medicine for centuries and is thought to have potential health benefits, including improving cognitive function and reducing the risk of cardiovascular disease.

Animals:

Fish oil - a rich source of omega-3 fatty acids such as eicosapentaenoic acid (EPA) and docosahexaenoic acid (DHA). Omega-3 fatty acids have been shown to have potential health benefits, including reducing inflammation, improving heart health, and cognitive function.

Collagen - a protein found in the connective tissues of animals, including humans. Collagen supplements have been marketed for their potential to improve skin health, joint health, and bone density.

Royal jelly - a substance produced by bees that is rich in vitamins, minerals, and a range of bioactive compounds such as proteins and fatty acids. Royal jelly has been used for centuries in traditional medicine and is thought to have potential health benefits, including reducing inflammation and improving immune function.

Microorganisms:

Probiotics - live microorganisms that provide health benefits when consumed in adequate amounts. Probiotics have been shown to have potential health benefits, including improving gut health, boosting the immune system, and reducing the risk of certain diseases.

Yeast beta-glucans - polysaccharides derived from the cell walls of yeast that have been shown to have potential health benefits, including improving immune function, reducing inflammation, and lowering cholesterol levels.

Lactic acid bacteria - a type of bacteria commonly found in fermented foods such as yogurt and kefir. Lactic acid bacteria have been shown to have potential health benefits, including improving gut health and boosting the immune system.

IV. Spirulina

Spirulina is a type of blue-green algae that is commonly used as a dietary supplement. It is a rich source of protein, vitamins, minerals, and antioxidants, making it an attractive nutraceutical. Here are some details about Spirulina:

Source: Spirulina is found in both salt and freshwater environments, and it is cultivated in many countries worldwide.

Name of marker compounds and chemical nature: Spirulina contains various bioactive compounds, including phycocyanin, chlorophyll, carotenoids, gamma-linolenic acid (GLA), and polysaccharides.

Medicinal uses and health benefits: Spirulina has been shown to have numerous health benefits, including boosting the immune system, reducing inflammation, lowering cholesterol levels, improving gut health, and protecting against oxidative stress. Additionally, it may help in the management of diabetes and obesity.

Potential side effects and precautions: While Spirulina is generally considered safe, some individuals may experience mild side effects such as gastrointestinal upset, headaches, and allergic reactions. It is recommended that pregnant or breastfeeding women, as well as those with autoimmune disorders, seek medical advice before taking Spirulina. Furthermore, it is important to purchase Spirulina supplements from a reputable source, as some products.

V. Soybean

Source: Soybean (Glycine max) is a legume native to East Asia and is now widely cultivated worldwide.

Name of marker compounds and chemical nature: Soybeans contain a variety of bioactive compounds such as isoflavones, saponins, phytosterols, and tocopherols. The isoflavones present in soybean, genistein, and daidzein, are structurally similar to the hormone estrogen and are classified as phytoestrogens. The phytosterols found in soybean are structurally similar to cholesterol and have cholesterol-lowering properties. Soybeans are also rich in protein, fiber, and unsaturated fatty acids.

Medicinal uses and health benefits: Soybean is known to have numerous health benefits such as reducing the risk of heart disease, cancer, and osteoporosis. The isoflavones in soybean have been shown to reduce hot flashes and other symptoms of menopause. The protein in soybean is a complete protein, containing all the essential amino acids required by the human body. Soybean protein has been shown to lower blood pressure, improve lipid profile, and reduce the risk of cardiovascular disease. Soybean is also rich in fiber, which promotes bowel regularity and reduces the risk of colon cancer.

Potential side effects and precautions: Although soybean is generally considered safe, some people may experience allergic reactions to soy products. People who are allergic to soybeans should avoid consuming them. Soybeans are also known to contain antinutrients such as trypsin inhibitors, which can interfere with the absorption of protein and other nutrients. However, the levels of antinutrients in soy products are generally low and can be reduced by cooking or processing. Soybean also contains phytoestrogens, which may interfere with the function of estrogen in the body. People with hormone-sensitive conditions such as breast cancer should consult their healthcare provider before consuming soy products.

VI. Ginseng

Ginseng is a popular nutraceutical derived from the root of various species of Panax. It is a common ingredient in traditional Chinese medicine and has been used for its medicinal properties for thousands of years. Ginseng contains various bioactive compounds, including ginsenosides, polysaccharides, and flavonoids.

Source and Chemical Nature

Ginseng is primarily sourced from the roots of Panax ginseng, Panax quinquefolius, and Panax notoginseng. It is commonly grown in regions of China, Korea, and Siberia. Ginsenosides are the main active components of ginseng and are responsible for its health benefits. These compounds belong to a class of triterpenoid saponins and are found exclusively in the Panax species.

Medicinal Uses and Health Benefits

Ginseng has been traditionally used for its adaptogenic properties, which are believed to help the body cope with physical and mental stress. It is also known to possess immune-modulating, anti-inflammatory, and antioxidant properties. Some of the reported health benefits of ginseng include:

Improving cognitive function and memory

Enhancing physical performance and reducing fatigue

Reducing inflammation and oxidative stress

Lowering blood sugar levels in diabetics

Improving erectile dysfunction and male fertility

Potential Side Effects and Precautions

While ginseng is generally considered safe for consumption, it may cause side effects in some individuals. These may include insomnia, nervousness, headaches, and digestive issues. It may also interact with certain medications, such as blood thinners and insulin. Pregnant and breastfeeding women, as well as individuals with certain medical conditions, should exercise caution and consult a healthcare provider before using ginseng.

VII. Garlic

Garlic is a member of the Allium family, which also includes onions and shallots. The bulb of the garlic plant is used for medicinal purposes. The primary active component in garlic is allicin, a sulfur compound that is produced when garlic is crushed or chopped. Other bioactive compounds in garlic include alliin, ajoene, and diallyl sulfide.

Garlic has been used for centuries for its medicinal properties. It has been shown to have antibacterial, antiviral, antifungal, and anticancer properties. Garlic has also been used to lower blood pressure, improve cholesterol levels, and reduce the risk of heart disease. It may also have anti-inflammatory effects and improve immune function.

Potential side effects of garlic include gastrointestinal problems, such as bloating and gas, and an increased risk of bleeding, especially when taken in large amounts or with certain medications. Garlic may also interact with certain medications, including blood thinners, and should be used with caution in these cases. Pregnant or breastfeeding women should also avoid taking garlic supplements without consulting a healthcare provider.

VIII. Broccoli

I. Broccoli is a member of the cruciferouegetable family and is known for its health-promoting properties. It is a rich source of vitamins, minerals, and phytochemicals, making it a popular choice as a functional food and nutraceutical.

II. Source, Marker Compounds, and Chemical Nature

Broccoli is a cool-season crop that is grown in many parts of the world. The edible parts of broccoli are the flower buds and the stalks. The primary marker compounds in broccoli are glucosinolates and sulforaphane. Glucosinolates are sulfur-containing compounds that are responsible for the bitter taste of broccoli, while sulforaphane is a phytochemical with potent anti-inflammatory and anti-cancer properties.

III. Medicinal Uses and Health Benefits

Broccoli has a range of medicinal uses and health benefits. Its high fiber content makes it beneficial for promoting healthy digestion and reducing the risk of constipation. Broccoli is also rich in antioxidants, including vitamins C and E, which help protect against cellular damage caused by free radicals. Sulforaphane, the primary marker compound in broccoli, has been shown to have anti-inflammatory properties and may help reduce the risk of chronic diseases such as cancer and cardiovascular disease. Additionally, some studies suggest that broccoli may have neuroprotective effects and may help improve cognitive function.

IV. Potential Side Effects and Precautions

While broccoli is generally considered safe for consumption, some individuals may experience digestive discomfort such as gas or bloating when consuming large amounts of cruciferous vegetables. Additionally, broccoli contains vitamin K, which can interfere with certain blood-thinning medications. Individuals taking these medications should speak with their healthcare provider before consuming large amounts of broccoli or other vitamin K-rich foods.

Overall, broccoli is a versatile and nutritious vegetable that can be consumed in a variety of ways, including raw, steamed, or roasted. Its health-promoting properties make it an excellent choice as a functional food and nutraceutical.

IX. Gingko

Ginkgo biloba is a tree species native to China, and its leaves have been used for medicinal purposes for centuries. The active compounds in ginkgo biloba leaves are flavonoids, terpenoids, and organic acids. The main flavonoids are quercetin, kaempferol, and isorhamnetin, while the main terpenoids are ginkgolides and bilobalide.

Medicinal uses and health benefits of ginkgo biloba include improving cognitive function, reducing anxiety and depression, reducing symptoms of premenstrual syndrome

(PMS), and improving blood circulation. Ginkgo biloba may also have neuroprotective effects and may help prevent or treat Alzheimer's disease, dementia, and age-related cognitive decline.

However, there are potential side effects and precautions to be aware of when using ginkgo biloba. Ginkgo biloba can interact with certain medications, including blood thinners and some antidepressants, and may increase the risk of bleeding. Ginkgo biloba may also cause gastrointestinal upset, headaches, dizziness, and allergic reactions in some individuals. Pregnant and breastfeeding women should avoid using ginkgo biloba.

X. Flaxseeds

Flaxseeds are tiny, golden or brown-colored seeds derived from the flax plant (Linum usitatissimum). They are a rich source of fiber, omega-3 fatty acids, lignans, and other bioactive compounds.

Marker compounds and chemical nature: The major bioactive compounds present in flaxseeds are lignans, which are phytoestrogens that have antioxidant and anticancer properties. Flaxseeds are also rich in alpha-linolenic acid (ALA), an omega-3 fatty acid that helps in reducing inflammation and improving heart health. Additionally, they contain soluble and insoluble fibers, vitamins, minerals, and other phytochemicals.

Medicinal uses and health benefits: Flaxseeds have been traditionally used for their laxative and anti-inflammatory properties. They are also believed to have a range of health benefits, including reducing the risk of heart disease, stroke, and certain cancers. The ALA present in flaxseeds helps in reducing the levels of LDL (bad) cholesterol and blood pressure. The lignans in flaxseeds have been shown to have anti-cancer properties and may reduce the risk of breast and prostate cancer. The fibers present in flaxseeds improve digestion, reduce the risk of constipation and irritable bowel syndrome (IBS), and promote weight loss.

Potential side effects and precautions: Flaxseeds are safe for most people when consumed in moderation. However, consuming large amounts of flaxseeds can cause digestive problems such as bloating, flatulence, and diarrhea. People with a history of bowel obstruction, intestinal ulcers, or Crohn's disease should avoid consuming flaxseeds as it may worsen their condition. Pregnant and breastfeeding women should also consult a healthcare provider before consuming flaxseeds, as they may affect hormone levels.

II

Phytochemicals as Nutraceuticals

Phytochemicals are naturally occurring bioactive compounds found in plants, which are not considered essential nutrients but have beneficial effects on human health. They are responsible for the color, flavor, and aroma of plant foods, and have been found to have a variety of health-promoting properties, including antioxidant, anti-inflammatory, anti-cancer, and cardiovascular protective effects.

Phytochemicals are classified based on their chemical structure and function, and include carotenoids, flavonoids, phenolic acids, glucosinolates, and others. These compounds are found in a variety of plant-based foods, including fruits, vegetables, grains, legumes, herbs, and spices.

The importance of phytochemicals in health promotion has been widely recognized in recent years, as research has demonstrated their potential to reduce the risk of chronic diseases such as cancer, cardiovascular disease, diabetes, and neurodegenerative disorders. Phytochemicals have been found to act through a variety of mechanisms, including reducing oxidative stress and inflammation, modulating cellular signaling pathways, and influencing gene expression.

Incorporating phytochemical-rich foods into the diet is a simple and effective way to promote health and prevent disease. Consuming a variety of colorful fruits and vegetables, whole grains, legumes, and herbs and spices is recommended to ensure a diverse range of phytochemicals is consumed. Additionally, phytochemical supplements are also available, but their safety and effectiveness may vary and should be used with caution.

Overall, understanding the definition and importance of phytochemicals in health promotion can help individuals make informed dietary choices and promote optimal health and well-being.

Carotenoids

Carotenoids are a class of phytochemicals that are responsible for the red, orange, and yellow pigments found in many fruits and vegetables. They are a family of over 600 naturally occurring pigments that can be divided into two main classes: carotenes and xanthophylls. Carotenes are hydrocarbons that contain only carbon and hydrogen atoms, while xanthophylls contain oxygen in addition to carbon and hydrogen atoms.

Carotenoids are found in a variety of food sources, including carrots, sweet potatoes, pumpkin, spinach, kale, tomatoes, watermelon, apricots, and mangoes. The absorption and bioavailability of carotenoids depend on a number of factors, such as food matrix, food preparation, and individual differences in digestion and absorption.

Carotenoids have been shown to have a number of health benefits and medicinal uses. For example, beta-carotene and alpha-carotene are converted to vitamin A in the body, which is important for vision, immune function, and skin health. Lycopene has been shown to have antioxidant properties and may have a protective effect against prostate cancer. Lutein and zeaxanthin are important for eye health and may help reduce the risk of age-related macular degeneration.

Other types of carotenoids include beta-cryptoxanthin, which is found in oranges, papaya, and peaches, and can be converted to vitamin A in the body. Astaxanthin is found in salmon and other seafood and has been shown to have anti-inflammatory properties.

III. Sulfides

A. Definition, Occurrence, and Chemical Nature

Sulfides are a class of organic compounds containing a sulfur atom bonded to two carbon atoms. They are found in various plants, particularly in the allium family, which includes onions, garlic, and shallots. The sulfur-containing compounds in allium vegetables are responsible for their characteristic pungent aroma and flavor. The two most important sulfides found in allium vegetables are diallylsulfide (DAS) and allyltrisulfide (ATS). These compounds are formed from the breakdown of the precursor compound alliin, which is converted to allicin upon tissue damage or crushing. Allicin then rapidly breaks down into a range of sulfur-containing compounds, including DAS and ATS.

B. Medicinal Benefits of Diallylsulfides and Allyltrisulfide

DAS and ATS have been found to possess various medicinal properties. They exhibit antioxidant, anti-inflammatory, and anti-cancer activities. Studies have shown that DAS and ATS can inhibit the growth of various cancer cells, including breast, colon, and prostate cancer cells. They can also induce apoptosis (cell death) in cancer cells, which is a key mechanism in preventing cancer growth. Moreover, DAS and ATS have been found to have cardio-protective effects, reducing blood pressure and cholesterol levels, which can contribute to the prevention of cardiovascular diseases.

C. Food Sources and Dietary Intake Recommendations

Allium vegetables, particularly garlic and onions, are the primary dietary sources of DAS and ATS. To obtain the potential health benefits of sulfides, it is recommended to consume allium vegetables on a regular basis. The World Health Organization (WHO) recommends a daily intake of at least 20 grams of allium vegetables per day, which is equivalent to about one to two garlic cloves or half an onion. However, it is important to note that excessive consumption of allium vegetables can lead to undesirable effects, such as bad breath, body odor, and digestive discomfort, especially for those who are sensitive to these compounds. Therefore, it is advisable to consume allium vegetables in moderation as part of a balanced diet.

IV. Polyphenolics

Polyphenolics are a diverse group of naturally occurring compounds that are widely distributed in plant-based foods. They are characterized by the presence of one or more phenolic rings and can be further classified based on the number of phenolic rings and the structural elements connecting them. The chemical structure of polyphenolics is responsible for their antioxidant properties, which have been linked to a range of health benefits.

Polyphenolics occur in various food sources, including fruits, vegetables, whole grains, nuts, and seeds. Berries, grapes, tea, and cocoa are particularly rich sources of polyphenolics. The polyphenolic content of foods can vary widely depending on various factors, such as the growing conditions, processing methods, and storage conditions.

The health benefits of polyphenolics have been extensively studied, and they have been shown to have potent antioxidant, anti-inflammatory, and antimicrobial properties. These properties make polyphenolics potentially beneficial for a range of health conditions, including cardiovascular disease, cancer, neurodegenerative diseases, and diabetes. Resveratrol, a type of polyphenolic found in grapes and red wine, has received particular attention due to its potential cardioprotective and anti-cancer effects.

Despite the potential health benefits of polyphenolics, it is important to note that their bioavailability can be limited, which can affect their efficacy in the body. Additionally, some polyphenolics may interact with certain medications, so caution should be exercised in individuals taking medication. Overall, increasing the consumption of polyphenolic-rich foods can be a simple and effective way to enhance overall health and well-being.

V. Flavonoids

A. Definition, Occurrence, and Chemical Nature

Flavonoids are a group of naturally occurring plant compounds that belong to the class of polyphenols. They are found in a wide range of fruits, vegetables, and herbs, and are responsible for the vibrant colors of many of these plant-based foods. Flavonoids are characterized by their chemical structure, which consists of two aromatic rings (A and B) connected by a three-carbon bridge (C). The arrangement and number of hydroxyl (-OH) groups and other functional groups attached to the rings and bridge determine the specific type of flavonoid.

B. Medicinal Benefits of Rutin, Naringin, Quercetin, Anthocyanidins, Catechins, and Flavones

Flavonoids have been shown to possess a wide range of health benefits, including anti-inflammatory, antioxidant, anti-cancer, anti-diabetic, anti-hypertensive, and anti-viral properties. Rutin, a type of flavonoid found in citrus fruits, buckwheat, and asparagus, has been shown to improve blood circulation, strengthen blood vessels, and reduce inflammation. Naringin, found in grapefruit and other citrus fruits, has been studied for its potential role in reducing cholesterol levels and aiding weight loss. Quercetin, found in onions, apples, and berries, has been shown to have anti-cancer properties and to reduce the risk of heart disease. Anthocyanidins, found in berries and other colorful fruits, have been associated with improved cognitive function and a reduced risk of type 2 diabetes. Catechins, found in green tea, have been studied for their anti-cancer and anti-inflammatory properties. Flavones, found in parsley, celery, and other herbs, have been shown to have anti-inflammatory and anti-cancer effects.

C. Food Sources and Dietary Intake Recommendations

Flavonoids are found in a wide variety of plant-based foods, including fruits, vegetables, herbs, and spices. Some of the best food sources of flavonoids include berries (such as blueberries, strawberries, and raspberries), citrus fruits (such as oranges, grapefruits, and lemons), apples, onions, broccoli, kale, tea, and red wine. The specific flavonoids present in these foods can vary widely depending on the plant species, growing conditions, and processing methods used. The recommended dietary intake of flavonoids has not been established, but incorporating a variety of colorful fruits, vegetables, and herbs into your diet can help ensure a good intake of these important phytochemicals.

VI. Prebiotics and Probiotics

A. Definition, Occurrence, and Chemical Nature

Prebiotics are non-digestible food components that selectively promote the growth and/or activity of beneficial bacteria in the gut, thus conferring health benefits to the host. On the other hand, probiotics are live microorganisms that, when administered in adequate amounts, confer a health benefit on the host.

Fructo oligosaccharides (FOS) are one of the most commonly used prebiotics, and they are naturally present in many plant-based foods such as asparagus, chicory, garlic, onion, and wheat. Lactobacillus is a type of probiotic that is naturally present in fermented foods such as yogurt, kefir, and sauerkraut.

B. Medicinal Benefits of Fructo Oligosaccharides and Lactobacillus

Fructo oligosaccharides have been shown to improve digestion, increase calcium absorption, and reduce the risk of colon cancer. They also have prebiotic effects, selectively stimulating the growth of beneficial bacteria in the gut such as Bifidobacterium and Lactobacillus.

Lactobacillus has been shown to have numerous health benefits, including improving immune function, reducing symptoms of lactose intolerance, and reducing the incidence and duration of diarrhea associated with antibiotic use. It also helps in the prevention of urinary tract infections and the reduction of cholesterol levels.

C. Food Sources and Dietary Intake Recommendations

Fructo oligosaccharides occur naturally in many plant-based foods and can also be consumed as supplements. The recommended daily intake of FOS varies from 4 to 20 grams depending on the specific application and individual requirements.

Lactobacillus is naturally present in fermented foods such as yogurt, kefir, and sauerkraut. It is also available as a supplement in the form of capsules, tablets, or powders. The recommended daily intake of probiotics varies depending on the specific strain and application.

VII. Phytoestrogens

A. Definition, Occurrence, and Chemical Nature of Phytoestrogens:

Phytoestrogens are a group of naturally occurring compounds found in plants that can mimic the activity of estrogen in the body. They are structurally similar to estrogen and can bind to estrogen receptors, but they are weaker in their activity than endogenous estrogen. Phytoestrogens are found in a wide range of plant-based foods, including legumes, soy products, flaxseed, and whole grains. There are several classes of phytoestrogens, including isoflavones, lignans, and coumestans, each with their distinct chemical structure.

B. Medicinal Benefits of Phytoestrogens:

Phytoestrogens have been studied for their potential health benefits, particularly for their ability to modulate estrogen activity in the body. Studies have suggested that phytoestrogens may reduce the risk of several chronic diseases, including cardiovascular disease, osteoporosis, and certain types of cancer. They may also alleviate menopausal symptoms, such as hot flashes and night sweats, due to their estrogenic effects. However, some studies have shown conflicting results, and more research is needed to fully understand the potential benefits and risks of phytoestrogen consumption.

Specifically, isoflavones such as genistein and daidzein have been studied for their potential anti-cancer effects, particularly in breast and prostate cancer. Lignans, found in flaxseed and whole grains, have also been associated with a lower risk of breast cancer. Phytoestrogens may also have a protective effect on bone health, as they have been shown to increase bone mineral density in postmenopausal women.

C. Food Sources and Dietary Intake Recommendations of Phytoestrogens:

Phytoestrogens are found in a variety of plant-based foods, with soy products being the most concentrated source. Other sources include legumes, flaxseed, whole grains, and some fruits and vegetables. The amount of phytoestrogens in these foods can vary widely, depending on factors such as growing conditions and processing.

The recommended daily intake of phytoestrogens varies depending on the individual's age, sex, and health status. However, studies have suggested that consuming up to 100 mg of isoflavones per day may have potential health benefits. This can be achieved through the consumption of soy products, such as tofu and soy milk, as well as legumes and other sources of phytoestrogens.

Overall, while phytoestrogens have shown promising health benefits, further research is needed to fully understand their potential effects on human health.

VIII. Tocopherols

A. Definition, Occurrence, and Chemical Nature of Tocopherols:

Tocopherols are a group of fat-soluble compounds with vitamin E activity, which have antioxidant properties. The term "tocopherol" is derived from the Greek words "tokos" meaning childbirth and "pherein" meaning to bear or carry. Tocopherols are commonly found in foods such as nuts, seeds, and vegetable oils. They are classified into four types: alpha-, beta-, gamma-, and delta-tocopherol, based on the number and position of methyl groups on the chromanol ring.

B. Medicinal Benefits of Tocopherols:

Tocopherols have been shown to have several health benefits, primarily due to their antioxidant properties. They help protect cells from damage caused by free radicals, which are unstable molecules that can cause oxidative stress and contribute to the development of chronic diseases such as cancer and cardiovascular disease. Tocopherols may also have anti-inflammatory properties and play a role in immune function.

Studies have suggested that tocopherols may have a protective effect against several types of cancer, including lung, prostate, and breast cancer. Additionally, they may help improve cognitive function and reduce the risk of age-related cognitive decline.

C. Food Sources and Dietary Intake Recommendations:

Tocopherols are found in a variety of foods, including nuts (especially almonds), seeds (such as sunflower and pumpkin seeds), and vegetable oils (such as olive, sunflower, and soybean oil). The recommended dietary intake for vitamin E, which includes tocopherols, is 15 mg per day for adults.

It is important to note that taking high doses of vitamin E supplements may have negative health effects, particularly in individuals with certain medical conditions or who are taking certain medications. It is generally recommended to obtain tocopherols and other nutrients through a balanced diet rather than supplements, unless recommended by a healthcare provider.

III

Introduction to Free radicals and its Measurement

1: Introduction to Free Radicals

Free radicals are highly reactive molecules that contain one or more unpaired electrons in their outer shell. These unpaired electrons make them highly reactive and unstable, which means they can easily react with other molecules and cause damage. Reactive oxygen species (ROS) are a type of free radical that contain oxygen atoms and are generated as a natural byproduct of metabolism in cells. ROS can also be produced in response to environmental factors such as pollution, radiation, and cigarette smoke.

Free radicals and ROS can cause damage to various cellular components, including lipids, proteins, carbohydrates, and nucleic acids. For example, free radicals can initiate a chain reaction known as lipid peroxidation, which damages cell membranes and can lead to cell death. They can also react with proteins, altering their structure and function, and with DNA, potentially causing mutations.

Despite their potential harmful effects, free radicals and ROS also play important roles in various physiological processes, including immune response, cellular signaling, and gene expression. However, when the production of free radicals exceeds the ability of cells to neutralize them with antioxidants, it can lead to oxidative stress and contribute to the development of various diseases, including cancer, cardiovascular disease, and neurodegenerative disorders.

Measurement of free radicals can be done by assessing the levels of lipid peroxidation products such as lipid hydroperoxide and malondialdehyde. Lipid peroxidation is a key indicator of oxidative stress and can be measured using various biochemical assays, including thiobarbituric acid reactive substances (TBARS) assay and high-performance liquid chromatography (HPLC). These measurements can provide insights into the extent of oxidative stress and help identify potential strategies for reducing the harmful effects of free radicals and ROS.

Free radicals are produced as a result of various biological processes in cells, such as mitochondrial respiration, inflammation, and metabolism. Mitochondria are organelles within cells that are responsible for producing energy in the form of ATP (adenosine triphosphate) via oxidative phosphorylation. During this process, electrons leak from the electron transport chain, leading to the formation of reactive oxygen species (ROS) such as superoxide anion, hydrogen peroxide, and hydroxyl radicals.

Inflammation is a complex biological response to harmful stimuli such as pathogens, damaged cells, or irritants. Inflammatory cells such as macrophages, neutrophils, and eosinophils produce ROS as a part of their defense mechanism against pathogens. The ROS produced by these cells can help to kill invading microorganisms; however, if not controlled, it can lead to tissue damage and chronic inflammation.

Metabolism also contributes to the production of ROS in cells. Aerobic metabolism generates energy in the form of ATP, but also produces ROS as by-products. Additionally, some enzymes involved in metabolic pathways produce ROS as part of their catalytic cycle. However, the body has several mechanisms to detoxify and scavenge these free radicals to maintain the balance between the production and removal of ROS.

Overall, the production of free radicals in cells is a normal and essential part of several biological processes. However, when the balance between the production and removal of free radicals is disrupted, it can lead to oxidative stress, which is associated with several diseases such as cancer, cardiovascular disease, neurodegenerative disorders, and aging.

Production of free radicals in cells:

Free radicals are produced as a result of various biological processes in cells, such as mitochondrial respiration, inflammation, and metabolism. Mitochondria are organelles within cells that are responsible for producing energy in the form of ATP (adenosine triphosphate) via oxidative phosphorylation. During this process, electrons leak from the electron transport chain, leading to the formation of reactive oxygen species (ROS) such as superoxide anion, hydrogen peroxide, and hydroxyl radicals.

Inflammation is a complex biological response to harmful stimuli such as pathogens, damaged cells, or irritants. Inflammatory cells such as macrophages, neutrophils, and eosinophils produce ROS as a part of their defense mechanism against pathogens. The ROS produced by these cells can help to kill invading microorganisms; however, if not controlled, it can lead to tissue damage and chronic inflammation.

Metabolism also contributes to the production of ROS in cells. Aerobic metabolism generates energy in the form of ATP, but also produces ROS as by-products. Additionally, some enzymes involved in metabolic pathways produce ROS as part of their catalytic cycle. However, the body has several mechanisms to detoxify and scavenge these free radicals to maintain the balance between the production and removal of ROS.

Overall, the production of free radicals in cells is a normal and essential part of several biological processes. However, when the balance between the production and removal of free radicals is disrupted, it can lead to oxidative stress, which is associated with several diseases such as cancer, cardiovascular disease, neurodegenerative disorders, and aging.

Damaging reactions of free radicals on lipids, proteins, carbohydrates, nucleic acids

Free radicals can cause damage to lipids, proteins, carbohydrates, and nucleic acids through a process known as oxidative stress. Lipids, such as cell membrane phospholipids, are particularly vulnerable to oxidative stress because they contain unsaturated fatty acids that are easily oxidized by free radicals. This leads to the formation of lipid peroxides, which can further propagate free radical reactions.

Proteins are also susceptible to oxidative damage by free radicals. Free radicals can cause amino acid side chains to undergo oxidation or can induce protein cross-linking. Such oxidative modifications to proteins can lead to a loss of protein function and aggregation, which can ultimately lead to the formation of protein aggregates that contribute to age-related diseases.

Carbohydrates, specifically monosaccharides, can also be oxidized by free radicals. This can lead to the formation of advanced glycation end products (AGEs), which are involved in the pathogenesis of several chronic diseases, including diabetes, cardiovascular disease, and Alzheimer's disease.

Finally, free radicals can cause oxidative damage to nucleic acids, particularly DNA. DNA damage can occur through direct interaction with free radicals or through indirect mechanisms involving oxidative stress-induced inflammation. This can lead to mutations, chromosomal aberrations, and ultimately contribute to the development of cancer and other age-related diseases.

Antioxidant Defense System

The human body has a complex antioxidant defense system to counteract the harmful effects of free radicals. This system consists of both enzymatic and non-enzymatic antioxidants.

Enzymatic antioxidants include superoxide dismutase (SOD), catalase, and glutathione peroxidase (GPx). SOD converts superoxide radicals into hydrogen peroxide, which is further degraded by catalase and GPx. Glutathione, a tripeptide composed of glutamate, cysteine, and glycine, is a non-enzymatic antioxidant that helps to regenerate other antioxidants, such as vitamin C and vitamin E.

Non-enzymatic antioxidants include vitamins C and E, carotenoids, and flavonoids. Vitamin C, also known as ascorbic acid, is a water-soluble antioxidant that works in the extracellular fluid to protect against free radicals. Vitamin E, a fat-soluble antioxidant, is located within cell membranes and protects against lipid peroxidation. Carotenoids and flavonoids are plant-derived antioxidants that have been shown to have a range of health benefits, including antioxidant and anti-inflammatory effects.

The antioxidant defense system is crucial for maintaining cellular and tissue health and preventing oxidative damage that can lead to aging and disease. However, when the production of free radicals exceeds the capacity of the antioxidant defense system, oxidative stress can occur, leading to damage to cells, tissues, and organs.

Importance of antioxidant balance in preventing oxidative stress

The balance between the production of free radicals and the antioxidant defense system is crucial for maintaining cellular and organismal health. Antioxidants are compounds that can neutralize free radicals by donating electrons or hydrogen atoms to stabilize them, preventing them from reacting with other molecules in the body.

The body has an intricate antioxidant defense system that includes both endogenous antioxidants (produced by the body) and exogenous antioxidants (obtained from the diet). Endogenous antioxidants include enzymes such as superoxide dismutase (SOD), catalase, and glutathione peroxidase. These enzymes work together to convert reactive oxygen species into less harmful compounds that can be eliminated from the body.

Exogenous antioxidants include vitamins such as vitamin C, vitamin E, and beta-carotene, as well as minerals such as selenium and zinc. These antioxidants can be obtained from a diet rich in fruits, vegetables, whole grains, and nuts, which are known to be high in antioxidants.

Maintaining a balance between free radicals and antioxidants is crucial for preventing oxidative stress, which has been linked to a variety of diseases including cancer, cardiovascular disease, Alzheimer's disease, and Parkinson's disease. In addition to a healthy diet, other lifestyle factors such as exercise, stress management, and avoiding exposure to environmental toxins can also help maintain antioxidant balance and prevent oxidative stress.

Measurement of Free Radicals (lipid hydroperoxides, malondialdehyde)

Lipid peroxidation is a chain reaction process that involves the oxidative degradation of lipids. This process leads to the formation of lipid hydroperoxides, which are highly reactive and can further damage cell membranes and organelles. Malondialdehyde (MDA) is a well-known biomarker of lipid peroxidation, as it is a major product of the decomposition of polyunsaturated fatty acid hydroperoxides. MDA can form adducts with proteins and nucleic acids, leading to cellular dysfunction and DNA damage.

Several methods can be used to measure lipid peroxidation products, including the thiobarbituric acid reactive substances (TBARS) assay, the fluorescent probes assay, and the gas chromatography-mass spectrometry (GC-MS) analysis. The TBARS assay is the most widely used method for measuring MDA levels, as it reacts specifically with MDA and other lipid peroxidation products to form a pink chromogen that can be quantified spectrophotometrically. The fluorescent probes assay is based on the reaction of fluorescent probes with lipid hydroperoxides, which results in a change in fluorescence that can be detected using a fluorometer. GC-MS analysis is a highly sensitive and specific method for detecting and quantifying lipid peroxidation products, including MDA.

Measurement of lipid peroxidation products can provide valuable information about the level of oxidative stress in cells and tissues. Elevated levels of lipid peroxidation products have been associated with various diseases, including cardiovascular disease, cancer, and neurodegenerative disorders. Therefore, measuring lipid peroxidation products can be useful for assessing the risk of developing these diseases and for monitoring the efficacy of antioxidant therapies

Protein carbonyls and DNA damage as markers of oxidative stress

Protein carbonyls and DNA damage are also used as markers of oxidative stress. Protein carbonylation is a chemical modification that occurs on the side chains of specific amino acid residues, particularly lysine and arginine. This modification can result in the loss of protein function, aggregation, and even degradation. The presence of carbonyl groups on proteins can be detected using various assays, such as the 2,4-dinitrophenylhydrazine (DNPH) assay or the Oxyblot assay.

DNA damage caused by oxidative stress can lead to mutations and genomic instability. One of the most commonly studied oxidative DNA lesions is 8-oxo-7,8-dihydroguanine (8-oxoG), which can lead to misincorporation of nucleotides during DNA replication and transcription. The level of 8-oxoG can be measured using various techniques, such as high-performance liquid chromatography (HPLC) or enzyme-linked immunosorbent assay (ELISA).

Overall, measuring protein carbonyls and DNA damage can provide valuable information about the extent of oxidative stress in cells and tissues, as well as potential biomarkers for disease risk and progression.

Techniques for measuring antioxidant capacity (ORAC, FRAP, DPPH)

The measurement of antioxidant capacity is essential to determine the ability of a substance to prevent or reduce oxidative damage caused by free radicals. Several methods have been developed to measure antioxidant capacity, including ORAC (oxygen radical absorbance capacity), FRAP (ferric reducing antioxidant power), and DPPH (2,2-diphenyl-1-picrylhydrazyl) assays.

ORAC is a widely used method for measuring antioxidant capacity. It measures the ability of a sample to scavenge peroxyl radicals generated during the oxidation of fluorescein. The reaction is monitored spectrophotometrically, and the area under the curve is used to calculate the ORAC value.

The FRAP assay measures the reduction of ferric iron (Fe^3+) to ferrous iron (Fe^2+) by antioxidants present in the sample. The reduction is monitored spectrophotometrically at 595 nm, and the results are expressed in micromoles of Trolox equivalents per gram or milliliter of sample.

The DPPH assay is based on the reduction of the stable free radical DPPH by antioxidants present in the sample. The reaction is monitored spectrophotometrically at 517 nm, and the results are expressed in terms of the concentration of antioxidant needed to scavenge 50% of the DPPH free radicals.

Overall, these assays provide a quantitative measure of the antioxidant capacity of a substance, and they can be used to compare the antioxidant activity of different compounds or food sources.

Sources and Effects of Free Radicals in Health and Disease

A. Sources of free radicals in the environment (pollution, radiation)

Environmental sources of free radicals include air pollution, water pollution, radiation, and chemicals in food and personal care products. Air pollution, such as from vehicle exhaust and industrial emissions, contains a variety of free radicals that can enter the body through breathing. Water pollution, such as from pesticides and heavy metals, can also contain free radicals that may be ingested. Radiation from sources such as X-rays and ultraviolet radiation can produce free radicals within the body, leading to DNA damage and oxidative stress. Chemicals in food and personal care products, such as preservatives and artificial dyes, may also contain free radicals that can contribute to oxidative stress when consumed or absorbed through the skin.

The effects of free radicals on health and disease are complex and multifactorial. High levels of free radicals and oxidative stress have been linked to a variety of chronic diseases, including cancer, cardiovascular disease, Alzheimer's disease, and diabetes. Free radicals can damage cell membranes, proteins, and DNA, leading to cellular dysfunction and death. In addition, free radicals can trigger inflammation, which can further exacerbate oxidative stress and contribute to disease progression.

However, it is important to note that free radicals also play important roles in normal physiological processes, such as immune function and cell signaling. The body has a complex antioxidant defense system to regulate and neutralize free radicals, and maintaining a balance between free radicals and antioxidants is crucial for overall health and well-being.

B. Effects of free radicals on various organ systems (cardiovascular, nervous, immune)

Free radicals can have detrimental effects on various organ systems of the body, leading to oxidative damage and dysfunction. The cardiovascular system is particularly vulnerable to oxidative stress, as it is constantly exposed to oxygen and susceptible to lipid peroxidation, protein damage, and DNA damage. This can lead to atherosclerosis, heart failure, and other cardiovascular diseases.

The nervous system is also vulnerable to oxidative stress, as it relies heavily on oxygen metabolism and has a high lipid content. Free radicals can cause oxidative damage to neurons, leading to neurodegenerative diseases such as Alzheimer's, Parkinson's, and Huntington's disease. Additionally, oxidative stress has been implicated in the pathogenesis of multiple sclerosis and other demyelinating diseases.

The immune system is also affected by oxidative stress, as it relies on reactive oxygen species for phagocytic activity. However, excessive free radical production can lead to impaired immune function and increased susceptibility to infection.

Overall, oxidative stress has been implicated in the pathogenesis of a wide range of diseases, including cancer, diabetes, autoimmune diseases, and chronic inflammatory conditions. Therefore, maintaining an appropriate balance between free radicals and antioxidants is crucial for maintaining optimal health and preventing disease

C. Role of free radicals in the development of chronic diseases (cancer, diabetes, Alzheimer's)

The role of free radicals in the development of chronic diseases has been widely investigated. Free radicals can lead to oxidative damage of cellular components such as proteins, lipids, and DNA, resulting in altered cell signaling, gene expression, and cell death. This damage can contribute to the development and progression of several chronic diseases, including cancer, diabetes, and Alzheimer's disease.

Cancer is characterized by uncontrolled cell growth and proliferation, and oxidative stress has been shown to contribute to the initiation and promotion of cancer. Free radicals can cause DNA damage and mutations, leading to the development of cancerous cells. Additionally, oxidative stress can promote inflammation, which has also been linked to cancer development.

Diabetes is a metabolic disorder that is associated with high levels of blood glucose. Oxidative stress has been shown to contribute to the development of diabetes by causing damage to pancreatic beta cells, leading to impaired insulin secretion. Free radicals can also contribute to insulin resistance by altering insulin signaling pathways in target tissues such as the liver, muscle, and adipose tissue.

Alzheimer's disease is a progressive neurodegenerative disorder characterized by cognitive decline and memory loss. Oxidative stress has been shown to play a role in the development and progression of Alzheimer's disease by causing damage to neurons, leading to dysfunction and cell death. Free radicals can also contribute to the formation of beta-amyloid plaques and neurofibrillary tangles, which are characteristic features of Alzheimer's disease.

D. Lifestyle modifications (healthy diet, regular exercise, stress reduction)

Oxidative stress can be detrimental to health and can lead to chronic diseases. Therefore, it is important to adopt strategies to reduce oxidative stress. Lifestyle modifications are one of the key ways to reduce oxidative stress.

A healthy diet that is rich in antioxidants can help to reduce oxidative stress. Antioxidants are found in many fruits and vegetables, as well as in nuts, seeds, and whole grains. Antioxidants help to neutralize free radicals and prevent damage to cells. A diet that is high in fiber and low in processed foods and saturated fats can also help to reduce oxidative stress.

Regular exercise is also an effective way to reduce oxidative stress. Exercise helps to improve circulation and oxygenation of tissues, which can reduce the production of free radicals. It can also help to increase the production of antioxidants in the body.

Stress reduction techniques such as meditation, yoga, and deep breathing exercises can also help to reduce oxidative stress. Stress can cause the production of free radicals in the body, which can damage cells and lead to chronic diseases. By reducing stress, the production of free radicals can be decreased, thus reducing oxidative stress.

Other lifestyle modifications that can help to reduce oxidative stress include getting enough sleep, avoiding smoking and excessive alcohol consumption, and reducing exposure to environmental toxins. By adopting these strategies, individuals can reduce the amount of oxidative stress in their bodies, which can improve overall health and reduce the risk of chronic diseases.

E. Antioxidant supplementation (vitamins, minerals, polyphenols)

Antioxidant supplementation has been suggested as a potential strategy for reducing oxidative stress and its associated health risks. Vitamins C and E, beta-carotene, and selenium are among the most commonly used antioxidants in supplements. These antioxidants work by neutralizing free radicals and preventing them from damaging cells and tissues.

Studies have shown mixed results regarding the effectiveness of antioxidant supplements in reducing oxidative stress and preventing chronic diseases. Some studies have shown that antioxidant supplementation can reduce oxidative stress markers and improve antioxidant capacity in the body. However, other studies have found no significant effects or even harmful effects of antioxidant supplementation, particularly at high doses.

One of the challenges with antioxidant supplementation is that the effects may depend on a variety of factors, including the type and dose of antioxidant, the timing and duration of supplementation, and individual differences in genetics and lifestyle factors. Additionally, some antioxidants may interact with certain medications or have negative effects when taken in high doses.

Therefore, it is important for individuals to consult with their healthcare provider before starting any antioxidant supplementation regimen. It is also recommended to obtain antioxidants from dietary sources, such as fruits, vegetables, whole grains, and nuts, rather than relying solely on supplements. A balanced diet rich in antioxidants, along with other lifestyle modifications, may provide a more effective and safer approach for reducing oxidative stress and promoting overall health.

F. (Pharmacological interventions (N-acetylcysteine, resveratrol, melatonin)

Pharmacological interventions can be used as a strategy to reduce oxidative stress. One such intervention is the use of N-acetylcysteine (NAC), which is a precursor of glutathione, a major antioxidant in the body. NAC can increase the levels of glutathione in the body and thus provide protection against oxidative stress. NAC has been found to be effective in reducing oxidative stress in a variety of conditions, including liver disease, respiratory diseases, and cardiovascular disease.

Another pharmacological intervention is the use of resveratrol, a polyphenolic compound found in red wine, grapes, and other fruits. Resveratrol has been shown to have antioxidant and anti-inflammatory properties and may help protect against oxidative stress. It has also been studied for its potential in reducing the risk of cancer, heart disease, and other chronic diseases.

Melatonin, a hormone produced by the pineal gland, is another pharmacological intervention that can be used to reduce oxidative stress. Melatonin is a potent antioxidant and has been found to be effective in reducing oxidative stress in a variety of conditions, including Alzheimer's disease, Parkinson's disease, and cancer.

It is important to note that the use of pharmacological interventions for reducing oxidative stress should be done under the guidance of a healthcare professional, as some interventions may interact with other medications or have potential side effects. Additionally, a balanced and healthy diet, regular exercise, and stress reduction should still be the first line of defense in reducing oxidative stress.

IV

"Free Radicals, Antioxidants, and Disease: Understanding the Role of Oxidative Stress in Health and Aging"

I. Introduction:

A. Recap of free radicals and their role in oxidative stress

Free radicals are highly reactive molecules that can cause damage to various biomolecules including lipids, proteins, carbohydrates, and nucleic acids. Reactive oxygen species (ROS) are a type of free radical that are produced during normal cellular metabolism as well as in response to environmental stressors such as pollution and radiation. The accumulation of free radicals and ROS can lead to oxidative stress, a condition in which the balance between oxidants and antioxidants is disrupted, resulting in cellular damage and dysfunction. Antioxidants are molecules that can neutralize free radicals and protect against oxidative stress.

B. Brief overview of diseases and disorders

Diabetes mellitus

Diabetes mellitus is a metabolic disorder characterized by elevated blood glucose levels. High glucose levels can promote oxidative stress and the production of free radicals, leading to cellular damage and dysfunction. This can contribute to the development of complications such as neuropathy, retinopathy, and cardiovascular disease.

Inflammation

Inflammation is a normal physiological response to injury or infection, but chronic inflammation can contribute to the development of various diseases such as arthritis, asthma, and inflammatory bowel disease. Free radicals and ROS can be produced during inflammation, exacerbating oxidative stress and contributing to tissue damage.

Ischemic reperfusion injury

Ischemic reperfusion injury occurs when blood flow is restored to tissues following a period of ischemia (lack of oxygen and blood flow). The reintroduction of oxygen and blood flow can lead to the production of free radicals and ROS, contributing to tissue damage and dysfunction.

Cancer

Cancer is a complex disease characterized by the uncontrolled growth and spread of abnormal cells. Free radicals and oxidative stress have been implicated in the development and progression of cancer, as they can promote DNA damage and mutations that contribute to the development of cancerous cells.

Atherosclerosis

Atherosclerosis is a condition characterized by the buildup of plaque in the arteries, which can lead to reduced blood flow and cardiovascular disease. Free radicals and ROS can contribute to the development of atherosclerosis by promoting inflammation, oxidative stress, and the accumulation of LDL cholesterol in the arteries.

Free radicals in brain metabolism and pathology

Free radicals and oxidative stress have been implicated in various neurological conditions such as Alzheimer's disease, Parkinson's disease, and stroke. These conditions are characterized by the accumulation of damaged proteins and oxidative stress in the brain.

Kidney damage

Free radicals and ROS have been implicated in the development of kidney damage and dysfunction, particularly in conditions such as diabetes and hypertension.

Muscle damage

Exercise-induced muscle damage can lead to the production of free radicals and ROS, contributing to oxidative stress and muscle dysfunction.

Other disorders involving free radicals

Free radicals and oxidative stress have been implicated in various other disorders such as liver disease, lung disease, and autoimmune disorders.

Free radicals theory of ageing

The free radical theory of ageing proposes that ageing is a result of the accumulation of oxidative damage to cellular components over time. This damage is caused by free radicals and ROS, which can lead to cellular dysfunction and death.

II. Free Radicals in Diabetes Mellitus

A. Introduction to Diabetes Mellitus

Definition and types of diabetes: Diabetes Mellitus is a chronic metabolic disorder characterized by high levels of blood glucose due to either the deficiency of insulin hormone or impaired insulin action in the body. The two main types of diabetes are type 1 diabetes and type 2 diabetes. Type 1 diabetes is an autoimmune disorder in which the immune system attacks and destroys insulin-producing beta cells in the pancreas, leading to a lack of insulin. Type 2 diabetes occurs when the body cannot effectively use insulin or produce enough insulin, leading to high blood sugar levels.

Pathophysiology of diabetes: The pathophysiology of diabetes involves a complex interplay between genetic, environmental, and lifestyle factors. In type 1 diabetes, there is a destruction of pancreatic beta cells, leading to an absolute deficiency of insulin production. In contrast, type 2 diabetes is characterized by insulin resistance, where the body's cells become resistant to insulin, and impaired beta cell function, leading to decreased insulin secretion. Both types of diabetes result in elevated levels of glucose in the blood, which can cause damage to various organs and tissues.

B. Role of Free Radicals in Diabetes Mellitus

Oxidative stress and its contribution to diabetes: Oxidative stress is a condition that arises due to an imbalance between the production of free radicals and antioxidant defense mechanisms. Diabetes mellitus is associated with increased oxidative stress, as evidenced by the elevated levels of oxidative stress markers, such as malondialdehyde, protein carbonyls, and advanced glycation end-products, in diabetic patients. Oxidative stress can contribute to the pathogenesis of diabetes by causing damage to pancreatic beta cells, leading to reduced insulin secretion, and impairing insulin signaling pathways in peripheral tissues, leading to insulin resistance.

Effects of oxidative stress on various organ systems in diabetes: Oxidative stress can also cause damage to various organ systems in diabetes. For example, in the cardiovascular system, oxidative stress can contribute to the development of atherosclerosis, a major complication of diabetes. In the nervous system, oxidative stress can cause damage to neurons and contribute to the development of diabetic neuropathy. In the kidneys, oxidative stress can lead to the development of diabetic nephropathy, a major cause of end-stage renal disease in diabetic patients.

C. Strategies for Reducing Oxidative Stress in Diabetes

Lifestyle modifications:

Lifestyle modifications, such as regular physical activity, healthy diet, and stress reduction, are effective strategies for reducing oxidative stress in diabetes. Regular exercise has been shown to increase antioxidant defense mechanisms and reduce oxidative stress in diabetic patients. A healthy diet rich in antioxidants, such as fruits, vegetables, and whole grains, can also reduce oxidative stress by providing the body with essential nutrients that scavenge free radicals. Stress reduction techniques, such as meditation and yoga, can also reduce oxidative stress by lowering cortisol levels.

Antioxidant supplementation:

Antioxidant supplementation with vitamins C and E, alpha-lipoic acid, and coenzyme Q10 has been shown to reduce oxidative stress and improve insulin sensitivity in diabetic patients. However, the optimal doses and duration of antioxidant supplementation are still under investigation, and excessive supplementation may have adverse effects.

Pharmacological interventions:

Pharmacological interventions, such as N-acetylcysteine and resveratrol, have been shown to reduce oxidative stress and improve insulin sensitivity in diabetic patients. N-acetylcysteine is a precursor of glutathione, a major antioxidant in the body, and has been shown to increase glutathione levels and reduce oxidative stress in diabetic patients. Resveratrol is a polyphenolic compound found in grapes and red wine and has been studied for its potential health benefits, including its antioxidant and anti-inflammatory properties. It has been shown to activate certain enzymes involved in reducing oxidative stress and to have potential protective effects against various diseases, including cancer, cardiovascular disease, and neurodegenerative disorders. However, further research is needed to fully understand the mechanisms of resveratrol's actions and its potential therapeutic applications

A. Introduction to Inflammation

Inflammation is a complex biological response of the body to harmful stimuli, such as pathogens, irritants, or damaged cells. It is a protective mechanism that helps the body to eliminate the harmful stimuli and initiate the healing process. However, if the inflammatory response is prolonged or excessive, it can lead to tissue damage and contribute to the development of various diseases.

B. Role of Free Radicals in Inflammation

Inflammation is associated with the production of reactive oxygen species (ROS) and reactive nitrogen species (RNS), which are generated by immune cells such as neutrophils, macrophages, and monocytes during the respiratory burst. These reactive species are important in the host defense against pathogens but can also contribute to tissue damage and inflammation when produced in excess.

ROS and RNS can damage cellular components such as lipids, proteins, and DNA, leading to oxidative stress and activation of pro-inflammatory signaling pathways. Inflammatory cells can also release cytokines and chemokines, which can induce oxidative stress and further amplify the inflammatory response.

C. Strategies for Reducing Oxidative Stress in Inflammation

Lifestyle modifications such as regular exercise, a healthy diet, and stress reduction can help reduce oxidative stress and inflammation. Antioxidant-rich foods such as fruits, vegetables, and nuts can provide the body with essential vitamins and minerals that act as antioxidants and reduce the damaging effects of free radicals.

Antioxidant supplementation can also be helpful in reducing oxidative stress and inflammation. Vitamins such as vitamin C, vitamin E, and beta-carotene, as well as minerals such as selenium and zinc, have been shown to have antioxidant properties and reduce inflammation.

Pharmacological interventions such as non-steroidal anti-inflammatory drugs (NSAIDs) and corticosteroids can also reduce inflammation by blocking the production of pro-inflammatory cytokines and chemokines. Additionally, natural compounds such as curcumin, resveratrol, and quercetin have been shown to have anti-inflammatory and antioxidant properties and can be used as potential therapeutic agents for reducing inflammation and oxidative stress.

III. Free Radicals in Inflammation

A. Introduction to Inflammation

Inflammation is a complex biological response of the body to harmful stimuli, such as pathogens, irritants, or damaged cells. It is a protective mechanism that helps the body to eliminate the harmful stimuli and initiate the healing process. However, if the inflammatory response is prolonged or excessive, it can lead to tissue damage and contribute to the development of various diseases.

B. Role of Free Radicals in Inflammation

Inflammation is associated with the production of reactive oxygen species (ROS) and reactive nitrogen species (RNS), which are generated by immune cells such as neutrophils, macrophages, and monocytes during the respiratory burst. These reactive species are important in the host defense against pathogens but can also contribute to tissue damage and inflammation when produced in excess.

ROS and RNS can damage cellular components such as lipids, proteins, and DNA, leading to oxidative stress and activation of pro-inflammatory signaling pathways. Inflammatory cells can also release cytokines and chemokines, which can induce oxidative stress and further amplify the inflammatory response.

C. Strategies for Reducing Oxidative Stress in Inflammation

Lifestyle modifications such as regular exercise, a healthy diet, and stress reduction can help reduce oxidative stress and inflammation. Antioxidant-rich foods such as fruits, vegetables, and nuts can provide the body with essential vitamins and minerals that act as antioxidants and reduce the damaging effects of free radicals.

Antioxidant supplementation can also be helpful in reducing oxidative stress and inflammation. Vitamins such as vitamin C, vitamin E, and beta-carotene, as well as minerals such as selenium and zinc, have been shown to have antioxidant properties and reduce inflammation.

Pharmacological interventions such as non-steroidal anti-inflammatory drugs (NSAIDs) and corticosteroids can also reduce inflammation by blocking the production of pro-inflammatory cytokines and chemokines. Additionally, natural compounds such as curcumin, resveratrol, and quercetin have been shown to have anti-inflammatory and antioxidant properties and can be used as potential therapeutic agents for reducing inflammation and oxidative stress.

IV. Free Radicals in Ischemic Reperfusion Injury

A. Introduction to Ischemic Reperfusion Injury:

Ischemic reperfusion injury (IRI) is a type of tissue damage that occurs when blood flow to an organ or tissue is disrupted, followed by restoration of blood flow. This type of injury is commonly seen in medical conditions such as myocardial infarction, stroke, and organ transplantation. IRI can lead to a series of pathological events, including oxidative stress, inflammation, and cell death, which can result in organ dysfunction or failure.

During the ischemic phase, the lack of oxygen and nutrients causes a decrease in ATP production, leading to cell membrane depolarization, intracellular calcium overload, and the production of reactive oxygen species (ROS). When blood flow is restored, the sudden influx of oxygen and nutrients can cause an additional burst of ROS production, which can further exacerbate oxidative stress and contribute to tissue damage.

B.Pathophysiology of ischemic reperfusion injury:

The pathophysiology of IRI involves a complex interplay between cellular, molecular, and inflammatory pathways. The extent of tissue damage and functional impairment is influenced by the duration and severity of ischemia, the degree of reperfusion injury, and the susceptibility of the tissue to oxidative stress and inflammation.

Understanding the mechanisms underlying IRI is critical for the development of effective strategies to prevent or treat this type of injury. Several interventions, such as ischemic preconditioning, pharmacological agents, and antioxidant therapy, have been studied as potential treatments for IRI. However, further research is needed to identify the most effective strategies for reducing oxidative stress and inflammation in IRI, and to develop new therapeutic approaches to prevent or mitigate tissue damage in this condition.

Role of Free Radicals in Ischemic Reperfusion Injury

Ischemic reperfusion injury refers to the damage that occurs to tissues or organs when blood flow is restored after a period of ischemia, which is the deprivation of oxygen and nutrients due to a lack of blood flow. This injury can occur in various organs such as the heart, brain, kidneys, liver, and intestines. The types of ischemic reperfusion injury depend on the severity and duration of ischemia, as well as the type of tissue or organ affected. Ischemic stroke, myocardial infarction, and acute kidney injury are some of the common examples of ischemic reperfusion injury.

Oxidative stress and its contribution to ischemic reperfusion injury

During ischemic reperfusion injury, the sudden reintroduction of oxygen to the ischemic tissue can lead to an excessive production of reactive oxygen species (ROS) and reactive nitrogen species (RNS), resulting in oxidative stress. ROS and RNS can cause damage to various biomolecules, such as lipids, proteins, and DNA, leading to tissue injury and cell death. In addition, oxidative stress can activate several pro-inflammatory pathways, leading to an inflammatory response that exacerbates tissue injury. Thus, the contribution of oxidative stress to ischemic reperfusion injury is significant and plays a crucial role in the pathogenesis of this condition

Effects of oxidative stress on various organ systems in ischemic reperfusion injury

Ischemic reperfusion injury can affect various organ systems in the body, including the heart, brain, liver, and kidneys. Oxidative stress resulting from the production of free radicals during ischemic reperfusion injury can cause damage to lipids, proteins, and DNA, leading to dysfunction and cell death in these organs.

Strategies for reducing oxidative stress in ischemic reperfusion injury include lifestyle modifications, such as regular exercise and a healthy diet, which can enhance antioxidant defenses in the body. Antioxidant supplementation, such as vitamins C and E, and polyphenols, can also help to reduce oxidative stress and prevent damage in ischemic reperfusion injury.

Pharmacological interventions, including N-acetylcysteine, resveratrol, and melatonin, have also shown promise in reducing oxidative stress and mitigating the effects of ischemic reperfusion injury. These interventions work by increasing the body's antioxidant capacity, reducing inflammation, and regulating cell death pathways.

Lifestyle modifications

Lifestyle modifications that can reduce oxidative stress in ischemic reperfusion injury include maintaining a healthy diet, regular exercise, and stress reduction. A healthy diet rich in fruits, vegetables, whole grains, and lean protein sources can provide the body with important antioxidants that can neutralize free radicals and prevent oxidative damage. Regular exercise has been shown to increase antioxidant activity and reduce oxidative stress. Stress reduction techniques such as meditation, deep breathing, and yoga can also be beneficial in reducing oxidative stress. In addition, avoiding smoking and limiting alcohol consumption can also help reduce oxidative stress and prevent further damage in ischemic reperfusion .

Antioxidant supplementation:

Antioxidant supplementation is another strategy for reducing oxidative stress in ischemic reperfusion injury. Antioxidants are substances that can neutralize free radicals and prevent them from causing damage to cells and tissues. Some commonly used antioxidant supplements include vitamin C, vitamin E, beta-carotene, and selenium.

Studies have shown that antioxidant supplementation can help reduce the severity of ischemic reperfusion injury by reducing oxidative stress and inflammation. For example, one study found that treatment with vitamin C and vitamin E reduced oxidative stress and improved cardiac function in patients undergoing cardiac surgery with cardiopulmonary bypass.

However, it is important to note that excessive antioxidant supplementation may also have negative effects on health, as some studies have suggested that high doses of certain antioxidants may increase the risk of cancer and other diseases. Therefore, it is recommended to consume antioxidants from a balanced diet rather than relying solely on supplements.

Pharmacological interventions:

Pharmacological interventions can also be used to reduce oxidative stress in ischemic reperfusion injury. N-acetylcysteine (NAC), a precursor to glutathione, is a commonly used antioxidant in this context. It has been shown to reduce oxidative stress and inflammation, and improve outcomes in various models of ischemic reperfusion injury.

Other pharmacological interventions that have shown promise in reducing oxidative stress and inflammation in ischemic reperfusion injury include resveratrol and melatonin. Resveratrol, a polyphenolic compound found in grapes and red wine, has been shown to have potent antioxidant and anti-inflammatory properties, and may improve outcomes in ischemic reperfusion injury. Melatonin, a hormone produced by the pineal gland, has also been shown to have antioxidant and anti-inflammatory effects, and may reduce the severity of ischemic reperfusion injury in various organs.

However, it should be noted that the use of pharmacological interventions in ischemic reperfusion injury is still an area of active research and there is no consensus on their optimal use or dosing. Further research is needed to better understand their mechanisms of action and potential side effects.

V. Free Radicals in Cancer:

Cancer refers to a group of diseases characterized by the uncontrolled growth and spread of abnormal cells in the body. These abnormal cells can form tumors, invade nearby tissues, and spread to other parts of the body through the bloodstream or lymphatic system. There are many different types of cancer, including carcinomas, sarcomas, lymphomas, and leukemias, among others. Carcinomas, which arise from cells that make up the skin, lining of organs, or glands, are the most common type of cancer. Sarcomas, on the other hand, arise from connective tissues such as bone, muscle, and cartilage. Lymphomas and leukemias are cancers that affect the blood and immune system.

Cancer can occur as a result of a combination of genetic and environmental factors, including exposure to toxins, radiation, viruses, and lifestyle factors such as tobacco use, poor diet, and lack of physical activity. The development of cancer involves a series of changes, or mutations, in the DNA of cells that can lead to uncontrolled cell growth and division. In some cases, these mutations can also result in the loss of the cell's ability to undergo programmed cell death, or apoptosis, which is an important mechanism for controlling the growth and spread of abnormal cells.

The role of free radicals in cancer is complex and not fully understood. On the one hand, free radicals can contribute to the development of cancer by causing damage to DNA and other cellular components, which can lead to mutations and other changes that promote uncontrolled cell growth. On the other hand, free radicals can also play a role in the body's natural defense mechanisms against cancer, such as by stimulating apoptosis in abnormal cells. The balance between these opposing effects is thought to depend on a variety of factors, including the type and stage of cancer, the patient's overall health and immune function, and other environmental and genetic factors.

Definition and types of cancer

Cancer is a complex group of diseases characterized by the uncontrolled growth and spread of abnormal cells in the body. Normally, cells in the body divide and grow in an orderly manner, replacing old or damaged cells. However, when genetic mutations occur in certain cells, they can start to divide and grow uncontrollably, forming a mass of abnormal cells known as a tumor. These tumors can be either benign or malignant.

Benign tumors are noncancerous and do not spread to other parts of the body. They are typically not life-threatening, although they may need to be removed if they are causing symptoms or are at risk of becoming malignant.

Malignant tumors, on the other hand, are cancerous and have the ability to invade nearby tissues and organs, as well as to spread to other parts of the body through the bloodstream or lymphatic system. This process of cancer cells spreading to other parts of the body is known as metastasis.

There are many different types of cancer, each with its own unique set of characteristics and treatment options. Some of the most common types of cancer include breast cancer, lung cancer, colorectal cancer, prostate cancer, and skin cancer. Other less common types of cancer include leukemia, lymphoma, and sarcoma.

Pathophysiology of cancer

Cancer is a complex disease that involves uncontrolled growth and spread of abnormal cells in the body. Normally, the body's cells divide and grow in a controlled way, with old or damaged cells dying off and being replaced by new cells. However, in cancer, this process goes awry, and cells begin to grow and divide uncontrollably.

Cancer can begin in any part of the body and is classified based on the type of cell that initially becomes abnormal. Some of the most common types of cancer include:

Carcinomas: cancers that start in the epithelial cells that line the outer or inner surfaces of the body, such as the skin or the lining of organs like the lungs, liver, or kidneys.

Sarcomas: cancers that start in the connective tissues, such as bone, muscle, cartilage, or fat.

Leukemias: cancers that start in the blood-forming tissues, such as the bone marrow, and result in abnormal blood cells.

Lymphomas: cancers that start in the lymphatic system, which helps fight infections and diseases.

The pathophysiology of cancer is complex and multifactorial, with various genetic, environmental, and lifestyle factors playing a role. Some of the key processes involved in the development of cancer include:

Mutations: Changes in the DNA of cells that can cause them to grow and divide uncontrollably.

Oncogenes: Genes that normally control cell growth but become overactive in cancer cells, leading to uncontrolled growth.

Tumor suppressor genes: Genes that normally help prevent cells from becoming cancerous but become inactive or deleted in cancer cells.

Angiogenesis: The process of forming new blood vessels that tumors use to grow and spread.

Metastasis: The process of cancer cells spreading from their original site to other parts of the body.

Understanding the pathophysiology of cancer is crucial in developing effective prevention and treatment strategies.

Role of Free Radicals in Cancer

The role of free radicals in cancer is complex and multifaceted. On the one hand, free radicals can damage DNA and other cellular components, which can promote the development of cancer. This is because mutations in genes that regulate cell growth and division are a common cause of cancer, and free radical-induced DNA damage can increase the frequency of these mutations. Additionally, free radicals can activate signaling pathways that promote cell growth and survival, which can also contribute to the development of cancer.

On the other hand, free radicals can also have anti-cancer effects. For example, free radicals can induce apoptosis (programmed cell death) in cancer cells, which can help to eliminate them from the body. Additionally, free radicals can activate immune cells that recognize and destroy cancer cells.

Overall, the role of free radicals in cancer is complex and context-dependent. While high levels of oxidative stress and free radical damage can contribute to the development of cancer, moderate levels of oxidative stress may actually have protective effects against cancer by inducing apoptosis and activating immune cells.

Oxidative stress and its contribution to cancer

Oxidative stress has been implicated in the pathogenesis of cancer. The accumulation of reactive oxygen species (ROS) can lead to DNA damage, protein modification, and lipid peroxidation, which can ultimately result in mutations and aberrant cell growth. ROS can activate signaling pathways that promote cell proliferation, survival, and angiogenesis, and inhibit apoptosis and immune surveillance, all of which contribute to cancer development and progression. Furthermore, ROS can induce genomic instability, a hallmark of cancer, by causing mutations and chromosomal abnormalities that promote tumor evolution and heterogeneity. In addition, ROS can also contribute to tumor microenvironment remodeling by modulating stromal cells, extracellular matrix, and immune cells, thereby creating a permissive niche for tumor growth and metastasis. Overall, oxidative stress plays a key role in cancer initiation, promotion, and metastasis.

Effects of oxidative stress on various organ systems in cancer

: Strategies for Reducing Oxidative Stress in Cancer

Cancer is a complex disease that involves uncontrolled cell growth and proliferation, which can cause damage to various organ systems in the body. Oxidative stress and the resulting damage caused by free radicals have been linked to the development and progression of cancer. Free radicals can damage cellular DNA, leading to mutations that can promote the development of cancer.

Strategies for reducing oxidative stress in cancer can be broadly classified into three categories: lifestyle modifications, antioxidant supplementation, and pharmacological interventions.

Lifestyle modifications: Several lifestyle modifications have been shown to reduce oxidative stress in cancer. These include regular exercise, a healthy diet rich in antioxidants, smoking cessation, and avoiding excessive alcohol consumption.

Antioxidant supplementation: Antioxidants such as vitamins C and E, beta-carotene, and selenium have been shown to reduce oxidative stress and may have a protective effect against cancer. However, the use of high-dose antioxidant supplements in cancer patients is controversial, as some studies have suggested that these supplements may interfere with chemotherapy and radiation therapy.

Pharmacological interventions: Several pharmacological agents have been shown to reduce oxidative stress in cancer. These include nonsteroidal anti-inflammatory drugs (NSAIDs), which can reduce inflammation and oxidative stress, and statins, which are commonly used to lower cholesterol levels but also have antioxidant properties. Other drugs that target oxidative stress pathways are currently being studied as potential cancer therapies.

In summary, reducing oxidative stress is an important strategy for preventing and treating cancer. While lifestyle modifications and antioxidant supplementation may be helpful, pharmacological interventions may be necessary in more advanced cases of cancer. However, further research is needed to better understand the complex role of oxidative stress in cancer and the most effective strategies for reducing it.

Lifestyle modifications

Lifestyle modifications can play an important role in reducing oxidative stress and preventing cancer. Some lifestyle changes that can help reduce oxidative stress and lower the risk of cancer include:

Maintaining a healthy weight: Obesity has been linked to increased levels of oxidative stress, so maintaining a healthy weight through a balanced diet and regular exercise can help reduce the risk of cancer.

Eating a healthy diet: Eating a diet rich in fruits, vegetables, whole grains, and lean protein sources can help provide the body with the necessary antioxidants and nutrients to combat oxidative stress.

Avoiding tobacco and excessive alcohol consumption: Tobacco smoke and excessive alcohol consumption can generate free radicals and contribute to oxidative stress, increasing the risk of cancer.

Getting regular exercise: Regular exercise has been shown to help reduce oxidative stress and lower the risk of cancer.

Managing stress: Chronic stress can contribute to oxidative stress, so managing stress through techniques such as meditation, deep breathing, or yoga may help reduce the risk of cancer.

Getting enough sleep: Sleep deprivation can increase oxidative stress, so getting enough sleep on a regular basis is important for overall health and reducing the risk of cancer.

Antioxidant supplementation

Antioxidants have been widely studied for their potential to reduce oxidative stress and prevent cancer development. In fact, some antioxidants have been shown to have chemopreventive effects in both preclinical and clinical studies. Examples of dietary antioxidants that have been investigated for their cancer-fighting properties include vitamins A, C, and E, as well as selenium and carotenoids. However, the effects of antioxidant supplementation on cancer development are complex and can vary depending on the type of cancer and the stage of disease. Some studies have even suggested that high-dose antioxidant supplementation may actually promote cancer development or interfere with cancer treatments, such as chemotherapy and radiation therapy. Therefore, it is important for individuals to consult with their healthcare provider before taking antioxidant supplements for cancer prevention or treatment.

Pharmacological interventions

Pharmacological interventions for reducing oxidative stress in cancer involve the use of drugs that act as antioxidants or free radical scavengers. These drugs include natural compounds such as vitamin C, vitamin E, and selenium, as well as synthetic compounds such as N-acetylcysteine (NAC), melatonin, and alpha-lipoic acid.

Vitamin C and vitamin E are well-known antioxidants that are commonly used as supplements to reduce oxidative stress in cancer patients. Selenium is a mineral that is also used as a supplement, as it is a component of several antioxidant enzymes. NAC is a derivative of the amino acid cysteine and acts as a precursor for glutathione, which is a major antioxidant in the body. Melatonin is a hormone that regulates sleep-wake cycles and also has antioxidant properties. Alpha-lipoic acid is a natural compound that is found in many foods and has been shown to have potent antioxidant properties.

Other drugs used in cancer treatment, such as chemotherapy and radiation therapy, can also increase oxidative stress. Therefore, some researchers are investigating the use of drugs that can target specific signaling pathways involved in oxidative stress and cancer development. For example, some studies have shown that targeting the Nrf2-Keap1 pathway, which is involved in regulating antioxidant response in cells, may be a promising strategy for reducing oxidative stress and cancer development. However, more research is needed to determine the safety and effectiveness of these interventions in cancer patients.

Free Radicals in Atherosclerosis

A. Introduction to Atherosclerosis

Atherosclerosis is a chronic and progressive disease characterized by the buildup of fatty deposits, cholesterol, and other substances within the walls of arteries. This leads to the thickening and hardening of the arteries, reducing blood flow to organs and tissues, which can result in various health complications, including heart disease, stroke, and peripheral arterial disease.

The development of atherosclerosis involves multiple complex mechanisms, including oxidative stress and inflammation. Free radicals, reactive oxygen species, and other oxidants play a crucial role in the initiation and progression of atherosclerotic plaques.

1. Definition and pathophysiology of atherosclerosis

Atherosclerosis is a chronic inflammatory disease characterized by the accumulation of lipids, cholesterol, and cellular debris in the walls of arteries, leading to the formation of plaques. The development of atherosclerosis is a complex process that involves multiple steps, including endothelial dysfunction, lipoprotein deposition, foam cell formation, smooth muscle cell proliferation, and matrix remodeling. The initial event in atherosclerosis is the dysfunction of the endothelial cells that line the inner wall of arteries, which can be triggered by various factors such as smoking, hypertension, and hypercholesterolemia. The dysfunctional endothelium promotes the infiltration of lipoproteins, particularly low-density lipoproteins (LDLs), into the sub-endothelial space, where they undergo oxidative modifications, generating oxidized LDLs (oxLDLs). The oxLDLs are recognized by scavenger receptors on macrophages, which engulf the modified lipoproteins and transform into foam cells, a hallmark of early atherosclerotic lesions. The accumulation of foam cells in the intima of arteries triggers an inflammatory response, involving the recruitment of immune cells, such as T cells and monocytes, and the production of cytokines and chemokines. The inflammation further promotes smooth muscle cell proliferation and migration, resulting in the formation of a fibrous cap over the lipid-rich core of the plaque. The unstable plaques are prone to rupture, leading to the formation of thrombi that can obstruct blood flow, causing ischemia and infarction in various organs, including the heart and the brain.

2. Risk factors for atherosclerosis

Role of Free Radicals in Atherosclerosis

Oxidative stress, which is characterized by an imbalance between the production of reactive oxygen species (ROS) and the antioxidant defense system, has been implicated in the development and progression of atherosclerosis. ROS can damage endothelial cells and promote the formation of foam cells, which are critical events in the development of atherosclerosis. ROS also contribute to the inflammatory response and oxidative modification of lipoproteins, which can lead to the formation of oxidized low-density lipoprotein (LDL) particles that are taken up by macrophages and lead to the formation of foam cells.

Furthermore, ROS can also promote smooth muscle cell proliferation and migration, which are key processes in the formation of atherosclerotic plaques. ROS can activate several signaling pathways, including the mitogen-activated protein kinase (MAPK) and nuclear factor-kappa B (NF-kB) pathways, which can induce the expression of genes involved in cell proliferation, inflammation, and apoptosis.

3. Oxidative stress and its contribution to atherosclerosis

Oxidative stress plays a critical role in the pathogenesis of atherosclerosis. Free radicals generated by various sources such as smoking, hypertension, diabetes, and hypercholesterolemia cause damage to the endothelial cells lining the arteries. This leads to a series of events, including the recruitment of inflammatory cells such as monocytes, and the secretion of cytokines and growth factors that promote the migration of smooth muscle cells to the intima layer of the arterial wall.

Once smooth muscle cells migrate to the intima, they proliferate and produce extracellular matrix, leading to the formation of a fibrous cap over the lipid-rich plaque. This fibrous cap is unstable and can rupture, leading to the exposure of the lipid-rich core to the blood and triggering the formation of a blood clot, which can lead to a heart attack or stroke.

Oxidative stress also promotes LDL oxidation, which further contributes to the formation and progression of atherosclerosis. Oxidized LDL can be taken up by macrophages and leads to the formation of foam cells, which are characteristic of atherosclerotic lesions.

4. Strategies for Reducing Oxidative Stress in Atherosclerosis

Lifestyle modifications: Making certain lifestyle changes can help reduce oxidative stress and prevent atherosclerosis. These include quitting smoking, regular exercise, a healthy diet that is low in saturated fats and high in fruits and vegetables, maintaining a healthy weight, and managing stress levels.

Antioxidant supplementation: Supplementing with antioxidants such as vitamin C, vitamin E, and beta-carotene may help reduce oxidative stress and prevent atherosclerosis. However, it is important to note that high doses of some antioxidants may have harmful effects and that more research is needed to determine the optimal doses and types of antioxidants.

Pharmacological interventions: Certain medications may also help reduce oxidative stress and prevent atherosclerosis. These include statins, which are commonly used to lower cholesterol levels, and angiotensin-converting enzyme (ACE) inhibitors and angiotensin receptor blockers (ARBs), which are used to treat hypertension and have antioxidant properties. Other potential pharmacological interventions being studied include antioxidants such as N-acetylcysteine, probucol, and coenzyme Q10.

Other interventions: Other interventions that may help reduce oxidative stress and prevent atherosclerosis include consuming omega-3 fatty acids, reducing exposure to environmental toxins, and reducing inflammation in the body. Additionally, some research suggests that interventions such as chelation therapy and ozone therapy may have antioxidant effects and may help prevent atherosclerosis, although more research is needed in these areas.

5. Lifestyle modifications

Lifestyle modifications can play a significant role in reducing oxidative stress and preventing the progression of atherosclerosis. These modifications include:

Quit smoking: Smoking is a major risk factor for atherosclerosis and also contributes to oxidative stress. Quitting smoking can help reduce oxidative stress and slow down the progression of atherosclerosis.

Exercise regularly: Regular exercise has been shown to improve cardiovascular health and reduce oxidative stress. It can also help improve blood flow and reduce inflammation, both of which are important in preventing atherosclerosis.

Maintain a healthy diet: A healthy diet rich in fruits, vegetables, whole grains, and lean proteins can provide the body with the necessary nutrients and antioxidants to reduce oxidative stress and prevent atherosclerosis.

Manage stress: Chronic stress can contribute to oxidative stress and increase the risk of atherosclerosis. Effective stress management techniques, such as meditation, yoga, or relaxation techniques, can help reduce stress and improve cardiovascular health.

Maintain a healthy weight: Obesity is a major risk factor for atherosclerosis and can also contribute to oxidative stress. Maintaining a healthy weight through diet and exercise can help reduce the risk of atherosclerosis and improve overall health.

6. Antioxidant supplementation

Antioxidant supplementation has been proposed as a potential strategy to reduce oxidative stress and prevent the progression of atherosclerosis. Some studies have shown that antioxidant supplements, such as vitamin E, vitamin C, and beta-carotene, can reduce oxidative damage to lipids and proteins in the vascular endothelium and decrease the risk of developing atherosclerosis.

However, other studies have produced conflicting results, and the use of high-dose antioxidant supplements has been associated with potential adverse effects. Therefore, it is important to consult with a healthcare provider before starting any antioxidant supplementation regimen, and to follow recommended dosage guidelines.

It is also important to note that dietary sources of antioxidants, such as fruits, vegetables, and whole grains, are generally considered safe and may offer additional health benefits beyond their antioxidant properties. Therefore, a balanced and varied diet is an important part of reducing oxidative stress and promoting cardiovascular health.

7. Pharmacological interventions

Several pharmacological interventions have been proposed to reduce oxidative stress and prevent atherosclerosis. These include:

Statins: Statins are cholesterol-lowering drugs that also have antioxidant properties. They inhibit the production of reactive oxygen species and increase the activity of antioxidant enzymes, reducing oxidative stress and inflammation in the blood vessels.

ACE inhibitors and ARBs: Angiotensin-converting enzyme (ACE) inhibitors and angiotensin receptor blockers (ARBs) are commonly used to treat hypertension. They also have antioxidant properties and can reduce oxidative stress in the blood vessels.

Vitamin E: Vitamin E is a potent antioxidant that can protect against oxidative damage to lipids in the blood vessels. It has been studied for its potential to reduce the risk of atherosclerosis, but the results have been mixed.

N-acetylcysteine (NAC): NAC is a precursor to glutathione, a powerful antioxidant. It has been shown to reduce oxidative stress and inflammation in the blood vessels and may have potential as a therapy for atherosclerosis.

Polyphenols: Polyphenols are a class of compounds found in many plant foods, including fruits, vegetables, and tea. They have potent antioxidant and anti-inflammatory properties and have been studied for their potential to reduce the risk of atherosclerosis.

Omega-3 fatty acids: Omega-3 fatty acids are found in fatty fish and some plant foods, such as flaxseeds and walnuts. They have anti-inflammatory properties and may reduce oxidative stress in the blood vessels. Omega-3 supplements have been studied for their potential to reduce the risk of atherosclerosis, but the results have been mixed.

It is important to note that while these interventions may have potential as therapies for atherosclerosis, more research is needed to determine their efficacy and safety. It is also important to consult with a healthcare provider before starting any new supplement or medication.

VII. Free Radicals in Brain Metabolism and Pathology

1. Overview of brain metabolism and its susceptibility to oxidative stress

Free radicals are highly reactive molecules that can cause damage to cellular components such as lipids, proteins, and DNA, leading to oxidative stress. The brain is particularly vulnerable to oxidative stress due to its high metabolic activity and high oxygen consumption. Oxidative stress has been implicated in the pathogenesis of many neurodegenerative diseases, including Alzheimer's disease and Parkinson's disease.

In Alzheimer's disease, beta-amyloid protein accumulates in the brain and forms plaques, which can trigger inflammation and oxidative stress. Oxidative stress can lead to the formation of more beta-amyloid plaques, creating a vicious cycle of damage. Additionally, oxidative stress can damage neurons and impair their ability to function properly, contributing to cognitive decline.

In Parkinson's disease, oxidative stress is thought to contribute to the degeneration of dopamine-producing neurons in the brain. Dopamine is a neurotransmitter that plays a critical role in movement and reward processing. Oxidative stress can damage these neurons and impair their ability to produce dopamine, leading to motor symptoms such as tremors and stiffness.

Overall, oxidative stress and free radical damage are thought to play a significant role in the development and progression of neurodegenerative diseases, making them an important target for therapeutic interventions.

2. How free radicals contribute to neurodegenerative diseases such as Alzheimer's and Parkinson's

Neurodegenerative diseases such as Alzheimer's and Parkinson's are characterized by the progressive loss of neurons in the brain. Free radicals and oxidative stress have been implicated in the pathogenesis of these diseases.

In Alzheimer's disease, free radicals can damage the structure and function of neurons, leading to the formation of beta-amyloid plaques and neurofibrillary tangles. Beta-amyloid plaques are formed by the accumulation of beta-amyloid proteins outside of neurons, which can cause inflammation and disrupt communication between neurons. Neurofibrillary tangles are formed by the accumulation of tau protein within neurons, leading to their death. Free radicals also promote inflammation and activate immune cells in the brain, leading to further damage and neuronal death.

In Parkinson's disease, free radicals can damage dopamine-producing neurons in the substantia nigra region of the brain, leading to their degeneration and death. This results in a deficiency of dopamine, a neurotransmitter important for movement control. Free radicals can also promote the formation of Lewy bodies, abnormal protein aggregates that are a hallmark of Parkinson's disease.

Overall, the damage caused by free radicals in neurodegenerative diseases can lead to progressive neuronal dysfunction and death, resulting in cognitive and motor deficits.

3. Strategies for Reducing Oxidative Stress in neurodegenerative diseases such as Alzheimer's and Parkinson's

There are various strategies for reducing oxidative stress in neurodegenerative diseases such as Alzheimer's and Parkinson's, including:

Lifestyle modifications: Maintaining a healthy lifestyle can help reduce oxidative stress in the brain. This includes regular exercise, a healthy diet rich in antioxidants, reducing stress, and getting adequate sleep.

Antioxidant supplementation: Antioxidants such as vitamins C and E, coenzyme Q10, and flavonoids have been shown to reduce oxidative stress in the brain. These antioxidants can be taken as supplements or incorporated into the diet through food sources such as fruits, vegetables, nuts, and seeds.

Pharmacological interventions: There are various medications that target oxidative stress in neurodegenerative diseases, including drugs that increase the production of antioxidants in the brain, such as N-acetylcysteine (NAC), and drugs that act as free radical scavengers, such as memantine.

Gene therapy: Researchers are exploring the use of gene therapy to increase the production of antioxidants in the brain. This involves introducing genes that code for antioxidant enzymes into the brain to enhance the brain's natural defense mechanisms against oxidative stress.

Stem cell therapy: Stem cell therapy is a promising approach for reducing oxidative stress in neurodegenerative diseases. Stem cells have the ability to differentiate into various cell types, including neurons, and can be used to replace damaged or dying neurons in the brain. Additionally, stem cells have been shown to have antioxidant properties and can secrete factors that promote neuronal survival and repair.

Current research on the use of antioxidants to prevent or treat neurodegenerative diseases

There is ongoing research on the use of antioxidants to prevent or treat neurodegenerative diseases such as Alzheimer's and Parkinson's. Some studies have suggested that antioxidant supplements such as vitamin E, vitamin C, and beta-carotene may help prevent or slow the progression of these diseases by reducing oxidative stress in the brain. However, other studies have shown mixed results and it is not yet clear whether antioxidant supplements are effective for preventing or treating these conditions.

In addition to supplements, researchers are also investigating the potential of antioxidant-rich diets, such as the Mediterranean diet, for reducing the risk of neurodegenerative diseases. There is some evidence to suggest that following a diet rich in antioxidants may help protect against Alzheimer's and Parkinson's by reducing oxidative stress and inflammation in the brain.

VIII. Free Radicals in Kidney and Muscle Damage

Kidney damage can occur due to various factors such as hypertension, diabetes, infections, autoimmune diseases, drug toxicity, and other conditions. The pathophysiology of kidney damage involves oxidative stress, inflammation, and cell death. Free radicals, particularly reactive oxygen species, contribute to kidney damage by damaging lipids, proteins, and DNA in renal cells. This results in inflammation, fibrosis, and eventually renal failure.

Muscle damage can occur due to physical injury, overuse, or genetic disorders. The pathophysiology of muscle damage involves oxidative stress, inflammation, and cell death. Free radicals can contribute to muscle damage by damaging lipids, proteins, and DNA in muscle cells. This results in inflammation, necrosis, and eventually muscle atrophy.

1. Role of Free Radicals in Kidney and Muscle Damage

Oxidative stress is a major contributor to the development of kidney and muscle damage. Reactive oxygen species (ROS) and reactive nitrogen species (RNS) generated by free radicals can cause damage to cellular components such as DNA, proteins, and lipids.

In the kidneys, oxidative stress can lead to damage of the glomerular basement membrane, tubular cells, and mesangial cells, which can impair renal function and lead to chronic kidney disease. In addition, oxidative stress can activate pro-inflammatory signaling pathways, leading to the release of cytokines and chemokines that further exacerbate renal damage.

In muscles, oxidative stress can cause damage to proteins involved in muscle contraction, such as actin and myosin, as well as impair mitochondrial function, which can lead to muscle weakness and atrophy. Oxidative stress can also activate pro-inflammatory signaling pathways, leading to the release of cytokines and chemokines that further exacerbate muscle damage.

Overall, free radicals and oxidative stress play a significant role in the pathogenesis of kidney and muscle damage.

2. Strategies for Reducing Oxidative Stress in Kidney and Muscle Damage

There are several strategies for reducing oxidative stress in kidney and muscle damage, including:

Lifestyle modifications: Lifestyle modifications such as exercise, a healthy diet, and avoiding smoking and excessive alcohol consumption can reduce oxidative stress and improve kidney and muscle health.

Antioxidant supplementation: Antioxidants such as vitamins C and E, beta-carotene, and selenium can scavenge free radicals and reduce oxidative stress. Studies have shown that antioxidant supplementation can improve kidney and muscle function in certain conditions.

Pharmacological interventions: Several drugs that target oxidative stress have been studied for their potential to reduce kidney and muscle damage. These include angiotensin-converting enzyme inhibitors (ACE inhibitors), angiotensin receptor blockers (ARBs), and statins, which have been shown to have beneficial effects on kidney and muscle function by reducing oxidative stress.

It is important to note that the effectiveness of these strategies may depend on the underlying cause of the kidney and muscle damage, and should be discussed with a healthcare professional.

IX. Free Radicals in Other Disorders

- **Brief overview of other disorders in which free radicals play a role, such as asthma and rheumatoid arthritis**

A. Free Radicals in Asthma

Asthma is a chronic respiratory disease characterized by airway inflammation, bronchial hyperresponsiveness, and reversible airflow obstruction. Free radicals play a role in the pathogenesis of asthma by causing oxidative stress and promoting airway inflammation.

Oxidative stress in asthma

Oxidative stress is increased in the airways of patients with asthma, as evidenced by elevated levels of reactive oxygen species (ROS) and reduced levels of antioxidant enzymes such as superoxide dismutase (SOD) and catalase. Oxidative stress contributes to the development and progression of asthma by damaging airway epithelial cells, activating inflammatory cells such as eosinophils and neutrophils, and promoting airway remodeling.

Effects of oxidative stress on asthma

Oxidative stress contributes to airway inflammation and bronchial hyperresponsiveness in asthma by several mechanisms:

Activation of inflammatory cells: ROS activate inflammatory cells such as eosinophils and neutrophils, which release cytokines and other mediators that promote airway inflammation.

Epithelial damage: ROS damage airway epithelial cells, disrupting the airway barrier and promoting the entry of allergens and irritants into the airways.

Airway hyperresponsiveness: ROS promote airway smooth muscle contraction, leading to bronchial hyperresponsiveness and airway obstruction.

Airway remodeling: ROS promote airway remodeling by stimulating fibroblast proliferation and collagen synthesis, leading to airway wall thickening and reduced lung function.

Strategies for reducing oxidative stress in asthma

Several strategies have been proposed to reduce oxidative stress in asthma, including:

Antioxidant supplementation: Antioxidant supplements such as vitamin C, vitamin E, and N-acetylcysteine (NAC) have been shown to reduce oxidative stress and improve lung function in patients with asthma.

Lifestyle modifications: Avoidance of environmental triggers such as tobacco smoke, air pollution, and allergens can reduce oxidative stress and improve asthma symptoms.

Pharmacological interventions: Several drugs have been shown to reduce oxidative stress in asthma, including inhaled corticosteroids, leukotriene modifiers, and beta-adrenergic agonists.

B. Free Radicals in Rheumatoid Arthritis

Rheumatoid arthritis (RA) is a chronic autoimmune disease characterized by joint inflammation, destruction of cartilage and bone, and systemic inflammation. Free radicals play a role in the pathogenesis of RA by causing oxidative stress and promoting inflammation.

Oxidative stress in RA

Oxidative stress is increased in the synovial fluid and tissues of patients with RA, as evidenced by elevated levels of ROS and reduced levels of antioxidant enzymes such as SOD and glutathione peroxidase. Oxidative stress contributes to the development and progression of RA by promoting synovial inflammation, cartilage and bone destruction, and systemic complications such as cardiovascular disease.

Effects of oxidative stress on RA

Oxidative stress contributes to RA by several mechanisms:

Synovial inflammation: ROS activate synovial cells such as fibroblasts and macrophages, leading to the production of pro-inflammatory cytokines such as interleukin-1 (IL-1) and tumor necrosis factor-alpha (TNF-alpha).

Cartilage and bone destruction: ROS promote the production of enzymes such as matrix metalloproteinases (MMPs) that degrade cartilage and bone, leading to joint damage and deformity.

Systemic complications: Oxidative stress promotes systemic inflammation and cardiovascular disease, which are common complications of RA.

Strategies for reducing oxidative stress in RA

Strategies for reducing oxidative stress in Rheumatoid Arthritis (RA) include:

Lifestyle modifications: Patients with RA can reduce oxidative stress by adopting healthy lifestyle habits such as regular exercise, smoking cessation, and maintaining a healthy diet rich in antioxidants.

Antioxidant supplementation: Antioxidant supplements such as vitamin C, vitamin E, and selenium can help reduce oxidative stress in RA. However, it is important to consult with a healthcare provider before starting any new supplements.

Pharmacological interventions: Some medications used to treat RA, such as disease-modifying anti-rheumatic drugs (DMARDs) and nonsteroidal anti-inflammatory drugs (NSAIDs), have antioxidant properties and can help reduce oxidative stress.

Nutritional therapy: Certain nutrients, such as omega-3 fatty acids and curcumin, have anti-inflammatory and antioxidant properties and may be helpful in reducing oxidative stress in RA.

Alternative therapies: Mind-body practices such as meditation, yoga, and acupuncture may help reduce oxidative stress and inflammation in RA.

It is important to note that while reducing oxidative stress may provide some benefits for individuals with RA, it is not a cure for the condition and should be used in conjunction with other treatments prescribed by a healthcare provider.

Mechanisms by which free radicals contribute to these disorders

Free radicals can contribute to asthma and rheumatoid arthritis through oxidative stress. In asthma, free radicals can damage the airway lining and trigger an inflammatory response, leading to bronchoconstriction and difficulty breathing. In rheumatoid arthritis, free radicals can damage joint tissue and trigger an immune response, leading to chronic inflammation and joint destruction. Additionally, free radicals can activate signaling pathways that contribute to the development and progression of these disorders.

X. *Free Radicals Theory of Aging*

The free radicals theory of aging suggests that aging and age-related diseases are caused by the accumulation of damage resulting from the normal metabolic processes of the body. During these processes, free radicals are produced, and if they are not neutralized, they can cause damage to cellular components such as DNA, proteins, and lipids, leading to cellular dysfunction and tissue damage. The accumulation of damage over time leads to a decline in organ function, increased risk of disease, and ultimately, aging.

Current research supports the role of oxidative stress in aging and age-related diseases, such as cardiovascular disease, neurodegenerative diseases, and cancer. Several studies have demonstrated that the levels of oxidative stress markers, such as lipid peroxidation and protein carbonyls, increase with age, and are associated with age-related decline in organ function.

Antioxidants have been studied as potential interventions to reduce oxidative stress and slow the aging process. Several animal and human studies have shown that antioxidant supplements, such as vitamins C and E, can reduce oxidative stress and improve age-related decline in organ function. However, the use of antioxidants as anti-aging interventions is still controversial, and more research is needed to determine the optimal doses, timing, and efficacy of these interventions.

In summary, the free radicals theory of aging suggests that reducing oxidative stress may be a promising approach to slowing the aging process and preventing age-related diseases. However, more research is needed to fully understand the mechanisms by which oxidative stress contributes to aging and to develop effective antioxidant interventions.

V

Food Laws, Regulations, and Claims: Ensuring Safety and Accuracy in the Food Industry

I. Introduction

Food laws and regulations are rules and guidelines established by governments and regulatory agencies to ensure the safety, quality, and labeling of food products. These laws and regulations are put in place to protect the health of consumers and prevent fraud or deception in the food industry.

Food laws and regulations cover various aspects of food production, processing, packaging, labeling, distribution, and marketing. They are enforced by government agencies such as the Food and Drug Administration (FDA), the Food Safety and Standards Authority of India (FSSAI), the Ministry of Health and Family Welfare, and other regulatory bodies.

The food laws and regulations may vary between countries, but they generally aim to achieve the following goals:

Ensure the safety of the food supply: Food laws and regulations are primarily intended to protect consumers from foodborne illness, contamination, and other hazards. These regulations set standards for the safe handling, processing, and storage of food products.

Ensure the quality of food products: Food laws and regulations establish standards for the quality of food products, such as nutritional content, composition, and labeling.

Prevent fraud and deception in the food industry: Food laws and regulations set standards for labeling and advertising of food products to ensure that consumers are not misled or deceived by false or misleading claims.

Promote fair competition in the food industry: Food laws and regulations are also intended to promote fair competition in the food industry by preventing unfair or deceptive practices that could give some producers an unfair advantage over others.

Food laws and regulations are essential to protect the public's health, ensure the quality and safety of food products, and promote fair competition in the food industry.

Importance of food safety regulations in protecting public health

Food safety regulations are critical to protecting public health. The consumption of contaminated or adulterated food can lead to various illnesses, including food poisoning, gastrointestinal diseases, and even death in severe cases. Therefore, food safety regulations are put in place to ensure that the food supply is safe for consumption.

These regulations help to prevent foodborne illnesses by setting guidelines for food production, processing, packaging, and labeling. They also establish standards for food quality and require that food producers and manufacturers comply with specific safety measures and procedures.

In addition to protecting public health, food safety regulations also have economic benefits. A foodborne illness outbreak can have severe economic consequences for the food industry, leading to lost revenue, decreased consumer confidence, and increased costs for healthcare and legal fees.

II. FDA (Food and Drug Administration)

A. History and purpose of the FDA

FDA or the Food and Drug Administration is an agency of the United States Department of Health and Human Services (HHS). The agency was established in 1906 under the Pure Food and Drugs Act, which prohibited the sale of adulterated or misbranded food and drugs. The purpose of the FDA is to protect public health by ensuring the safety and efficacy of food, drugs, medical devices, cosmetics, and other products that are regulated by the agency.

Over the years, the FDA has evolved and expanded its responsibilities, and now plays a critical role in regulating a wide range of products that are consumed by the public. The agency is responsible for reviewing and approving new drugs and medical devices, monitoring the safety and effectiveness of marketed products, ensuring the safety of the food supply, and regulating the manufacture and labeling of cosmetics and other consumer products. The FDA also enforces laws related to tobacco products and dietary supplements.

B. FDA regulations and guidelines for food safety

The FDA is responsible for ensuring the safety of the U.S. food supply and enforcing laws and regulations related to food safety. The agency has established a number of regulations and guidelines to help ensure that the food supply is safe for consumption. Some of these regulations and guidelines include:

Food labeling requirements:

The FDA has established strict guidelines for food labeling, which include requirements for the listing of ingredients, nutritional information, and allergen warnings.

Good Manufacturing Practices (GMPs):

GMPs are guidelines for the manufacturing of food products that help to ensure their safety and quality. These guidelines cover everything from the cleanliness of manufacturing facilities to the testing of finished products.

Hazard Analysis and Critical Control Points (HACCP): HACCP is a system of food safety management that identifies potential hazards in food production and establishes controls to prevent their occurrence. The FDA requires HACCP plans for seafood and juice processing facilities.

Food Additive Regulations:

The FDA regulates the use of food additives, which are substances added to food to enhance its flavor, texture, or appearance. The agency ensures that food additives are safe for consumption and do not pose a risk to public health.

Import regulations:

The FDA regulates imported food products to ensure that they meet U.S. food safety standards.

Foodborne illness outbreak investigations:

The FDA investigates outbreaks of foodborne illness to identify the source of the contamination and prevent further spread of the illness.

C. FDA enforcement of food safety regulations

The FDA enforces food safety regulations through a variety of means, including inspections, recalls, and legal actions. Inspections are conducted regularly to ensure that food manufacturers and processors comply with FDA regulations and guidelines. If a violation is found, the FDA may issue a warning letter, demand a recall of the product, or take legal action against the manufacturer.

The FDA also maintains a reporting system called the Safety Reporting Portal where consumers and healthcare professionals can report adverse events related to food products, such as illness or allergic reactions. The FDA uses this information to identify potential safety concerns and take action to protect public health.

In addition, the FDA works closely with other government agencies, such as the U.S. Department of Agriculture (USDA) and the Environmental Protection Agency (EPA), to address food safety issues that may arise throughout the food production and distribution chain.

III. FPO (Food Products Order)

A. Overview of the FPO

Food Products Order (FPO) is an order formulated under Section 3 of the Essential Commodities Act, 1955, to regulate the quality and safety of certain food products in India. The FPO was enacted in 1955 and applies to food products, including milk and milk products, edible oils, fruits and vegetables, meat and meat products, and certain other commodities. The FPO is enforced by the Food Safety and Standards Authority of India (FSSAI), which is responsible for ensuring that the food products are safe, wholesome, and of the prescribed quality.

The FPO specifies the standards for the quality and safety of food products, including the permitted levels of contaminants, the composition of food products, and the labeling requirements. The FPO also provides for the establishment of food testing laboratories to analyze the quality and safety of food products. The FSSAI is responsible for monitoring compliance with the FPO and taking enforcement actions against non-compliant food products.

B. FPO regulations and guidelines for food safety

The Food Products Order (FPO) in India is a set of regulations that govern the manufacture, distribution, storage, and sale of food products in the country. The order was first introduced in 1955 and has been revised several times since then to keep up with changing times and food safety standards.

The FPO outlines various standards and regulations for different categories of food products, including milk and milk products, meat and meat products, fish and fish products, fruit and vegetable products, and packaged drinking water, among others. The standards include parameters such as composition, quality, safety, and labeling requirements.

The FPO also establishes a system for licensing and registration of food businesses, including food manufacturers, processors, and distributors. Food businesses are required to comply with the FPO regulations and obtain the necessary licenses and registrations to operate legally in India.

The FPO is enforced by the Food Safety and Standards Authority of India (FSSAI), which is responsible for ensuring compliance with the regulations and standards set by the FPO. The FSSAI conducts regular inspections and audits of food businesses to ensure that they are adhering to the standards and regulations set by the FPO. Non-compliance with FPO regulations can result in penalties and legal action by the authorities.

C. FPO enforcement of food safety regulations

The FPO is enforced by the Food Safety and Standards Authority of India (FSSAI), which is responsible for ensuring that all food products comply with FPO regulations. The FSSAI carries out inspections and testing of food products to ensure compliance with the FPO, and has the authority to impose penalties and initiate legal action against non-compliant food businesses. In addition to inspections and testing, the FSSAI also provides guidance and training to food businesses to help them understand and comply with FPO regulations.

IV. MPO (Meat Products Order)

A. Overview of the MPO

The Meat Products Order (MPO) is a set of regulations in India that establishes standards for the production, processing, and packaging of meat and meat products. The order was established in 1973 by the Ministry of Food and Agriculture and applies to all meat products produced or imported in India.

The MPO sets standards for various aspects of meat production, including animal husbandry, transportation, slaughter, processing, and packaging. The order also establishes guidelines for the use of food additives, preservatives, and colorants in meat products.

The purpose of the MPO is to ensure that meat products sold in India are safe for human consumption and meet certain quality standards. The order is enforced by the Food Safety and Standards Authority of India (FSSAI) and violators can face legal action.

B. MPO regulations and guidelines for food safety

The Meat Products Order (MPO) provides regulations and guidelines for food safety related to meat and meat products. It sets standards for the hygienic production, processing, storage, and transportation of meat and meat products to ensure that they are safe for human consumption.

The MPO establishes requirements for the inspection of meat products and the licensing of establishments that produce, process, and distribute meat products. It also provides guidelines for the labeling of meat products to ensure that consumers have accurate and complete information about the products they purchase.

The MPO requires that all meat products be produced, processed, and transported in accordance with Good Manufacturing Practices (GMPs) to ensure that they are free from harmful contaminants and are safe for human consumption. It also requires that all meat products be inspected by trained and licensed inspectors to ensure that they meet the established standards for safety and quality.

Overall, the MPO aims to protect public health by ensuring that meat products are produced and distributed in a safe and hygienic manner, and that consumers have accurate information about the products they purchase.

C. MPO enforcement of food safety regulations

The enforcement of MPO regulations and guidelines for food safety is the responsibility of the Food Safety and Inspection Service (FSIS) of the United States Department of Agriculture (USDA). The FSIS is responsible for ensuring that all meat, poultry, and processed egg products produced in federally inspected establishments are safe, wholesome, and accurately labeled.

The FSIS enforces the MPO regulations through a combination of inspections, testing, and enforcement actions. Inspectors visit slaughterhouses and processing plants on a daily basis to ensure that all aspects of the production process, from the handling of live animals to the processing and packaging of meat products, are in compliance with MPO regulations.

The FSIS also conducts laboratory testing to ensure that meat products are free from harmful contaminants such as bacteria, viruses, and chemical residues. If a violation of MPO regulations is found, the FSIS may take enforcement actions, such as suspending or revoking a facility's inspection, seizing and condemning product, or prosecuting the responsible parties.

V. AGMARK

A. Definition and purpose of AGMARK

AGMARK stands for Agricultural Marketing. It is a quality certification mark given by the Directorate of Marketing and Inspection, Ministry of Agriculture, Government of India to agricultural products. The main purpose of AGMARK is to provide quality assurance to agricultural products and promote fair trading practices in the market.

The AGMARK certification ensures that the product meets the minimum quality standards set by the government in terms of grading, packaging, labeling, and storage. This helps in building the confidence of the consumers and also helps in promoting exports of agricultural products. AGMARK is applicable to various agricultural products like fruits, vegetables, cereals, pulses, spices, honey, and other products.

B. AGMARK regulations and guidelines for food safety

AGMARK is a certification mark used in India on agricultural products. It is a voluntary scheme that provides quality standards for agricultural products such as fruits, vegetables, and cereals. The purpose of AGMARK is to ensure that the agricultural products sold in the market are of good quality and meet the prescribed standards.

AGMARK has established guidelines and regulations for various agricultural products, including the following:

Quality standards: AGMARK has prescribed quality standards for agricultural products. These standards cover parameters such as size, shape, color, texture, and flavor.

Packaging and labeling: AGMARK has established guidelines for packaging and labeling of agricultural products. These guidelines ensure that the products are properly labeled with information such as the name of the product, net weight, date of packing, and expiry date.

Sampling and testing: AGMARK has established procedures for sampling and testing of agricultural products. These procedures ensure that the products meet the prescribed quality standards.

Certification: AGMARK provides certification to the agricultural products that meet the prescribed quality standards. This certification serves as an assurance to the consumers that the product is of good quality and meets the prescribed standards.

C. AGMARK enforcement of food safety regulations

As AGMARK is a voluntary certification system in India, there is no formal enforcement mechanism for ensuring compliance with its regulations and guidelines. However, the Agricultural Produce (Grading and Marking) Act, 1937 provides legal backing for AGMARK and empowers the government to take action against those who use false or misleading marks. Additionally, the AGMARK certification is issued by the Directorate of Marketing and Inspection, which conducts periodic inspections to ensure that the certified products continue to meet the prescribed standards.

VI. HACCP (Hazard Analysis and Critical Control Points)

A. Definition and purpose of HACCP

HACCP stands for Hazard Analysis and Critical Control Points. It is a systematic approach to food safety management that aims to prevent hazards, such as chemical, physical, or biological, from occurring in food production processes. The purpose of HACCP is to identify and control potential hazards at critical points in the food production process to ensure that the food is safe for human consumption.

B. Seven principles of HACCP

There are seven principles of HACCP that form the basis of its implementation:

Conduct a hazard analysis: The first step is to identify and evaluate potential hazards associated with the food production process.

Determine the critical control points (CCPs): The CCPs are the points in the process where hazards can be prevented, eliminated, or reduced to an acceptable level.

Establish critical limits: Critical limits are the maximum and minimum values for each CCP that must be maintained to ensure that hazards are controlled.

Implement monitoring procedures: Monitoring procedures are used to ensure that CCPs are under control and that critical limits are being met.

Establish corrective actions: Corrective actions are taken when monitoring procedures indicate that a CCP is not under control or that a critical limit has been exceeded.

Implement verification procedures: Verification procedures are used to ensure that the HACCP system is working effectively.

Establish record-keeping and documentation procedures: Record-keeping and documentation procedures are necessary to demonstrate that the HACCP system is working effectively and to facilitate regulatory inspections.

C. Importance of HACCP in food safety

HACCP is an important tool for ensuring food safety because it focuses on preventing hazards rather than reacting to them after they have occurred. By identifying and controlling hazards at critical points in the production process, HACCP can help to prevent foodborne illnesses, reduce the risk of product recalls, and improve the overall quality of food products. HACCP is also a legal requirement in many countries, and compliance with HACCP regulations is often a prerequisite for selling food products in international markets.

VII. GMPs (Good Manufacturing Practices) on Food Safety

A. Definition and purpose of GMPs

Good Manufacturing Practices (GMPs) are a set of guidelines established by regulatory agencies to ensure that food products are consistently manufactured and controlled according to quality standards. GMPs are designed to reduce the risk of contamination, adulteration, and errors during the manufacturing process, and ensure that products are safe for consumption.

B. GMPs regulations and guidelines for food safety

GMPs cover a wide range of topics related to food safety, including personnel, premises, equipment, production, quality control, and record keeping. Some specific regulations and guidelines for food safety under GMPs include:

Personnel: GMPs require that food manufacturing facilities have trained personnel who understand the principles of food hygiene, sanitation, and safety. Employees must be trained in proper hand hygiene, the use of protective clothing, and personal hygiene practices to prevent contamination of food products.

Premises: GMPs require that food manufacturing facilities be designed, constructed, and maintained to minimize the risk of contamination. This includes proper ventilation, lighting, and pest control measures. Facilities must also have appropriate sanitation procedures in place, including the regular cleaning and disinfection of all surfaces and equipment.

Equipment: GMPs require that all equipment used in the manufacturing process be properly designed, installed, and maintained to prevent contamination. This includes the use of food-grade materials, regular maintenance and cleaning, and proper calibration and validation of equipment.

Production: GMPs require that food products are manufactured according to established procedures and specifications. This includes monitoring and controlling critical parameters, such as temperature, humidity, and pH, and ensuring that raw materials and ingredients are properly stored, handled, and labeled.

Quality control: GMPs require that food manufacturers establish and maintain a quality control system to ensure that products meet established specifications and standards. This includes regular testing and analysis of products and ingredients, and proper record keeping.

C. GMPs enforcement of food safety regulations

GMPs are enforced by regulatory agencies, such as the FDA and USDA, through inspections and audits of food manufacturing facilities. If a facility is found to be in violation of GMPs, regulatory agencies can take a variety of actions, such as issuing warning letters, seizing products, or even initiating criminal proceedings. Food manufacturers must take GMPs seriously and ensure that they are in compliance to avoid regulatory action and protect public health.

VIII. Adulteration of Foods

A. Definition of food adulteration

Food adulteration refers to the addition or removal of substances to or from food, intentionally or unintentionally, which makes the food impure, unsafe, or inferior in quality. Adulterants may include substances such as chemicals, biological agents, or other substances that are not approved for use in food, or the use of approved substances in excess or inappropriate ways. Adulteration can occur at any stage of the food production process, from raw materials to finished products. Adulterated foods can pose serious health risks to consumers, and therefore, food adulteration is a major concern in food safety regulations.

B. Types of food adulteration:

intentional food adulteration

Intentional food adulteration refers to the deliberate addition or removal of substances from food products for economic gain or other fraudulent purposes. Some examples of intentional adulteration include adding water or other cheap ingredients to bulk up a food product, replacing a more expensive ingredient with a cheaper substitute, or using chemicals to enhance the appearance of a food product.

The motivations for intentional food adulteration can vary widely, but often involve financial gain. Adulterated food products can be sold at a lower cost, which allows for higher profits for the manufacturer or seller. In some cases, the adulteration is done to conceal poor quality or spoilage of the food product. In others, the adulteration is done to intentionally deceive consumers about the contents of the product.

Intentional food adulteration can have serious consequences for public health and safety. For example, the addition of harmful chemicals or substances to food can cause illness, allergic reactions, or even death. The use of unapproved food additives or the presence of allergens that are not disclosed on the label can also pose a risk to consumers with food allergies.

To prevent intentional food adulteration, regulatory agencies have implemented various measures, including food safety inspections, testing, and monitoring programs. Additionally, the implementation of strict regulations and penalties for adulteration can act as a deterrent to those who may be tempted to engage in this fraudulent behavior. Companies can also take steps to prevent intentional adulteration by implementing internal quality control measures, conducting regular testing of ingredients and finished products, and maintaining strict supplier requirements. Consumers can also play a role in preventing intentional food adulteration by being vigilant about the foods they consume and reporting any suspicious activity to regulatory agencies.

Unintentional food adulteration

Unintentional food adulteration refers to the contamination of food with harmful substances that are not added to it deliberately. It can occur during the production, processing, packaging, transportation, or storage of food. Some examples of unintentional food adulteration include:

Presence of environmental contaminants: Food can be contaminated with environmental pollutants, such as heavy metals, pesticides, and industrial chemicals. These contaminants can enter the food chain through the soil, air, or water.

Cross-contamination: This occurs when harmful microorganisms, such as bacteria or viruses, are transferred from one food product to another during processing, handling, or preparation.

Packaging materials: Chemicals from packaging materials, such as plastic or paper, can leach into food and contaminate it.

Unintentional food adulteration can be caused by various factors, including:

Poor sanitation and hygiene practices: Poor sanitation and hygiene practices during food production, processing, handling, or preparation can lead to the contamination of food with harmful substances.

Lack of quality control: The absence of quality control measures in food production and processing can lead to unintentional contamination.

Inadequate storage conditions: Improper storage conditions, such as temperature and humidity, can lead to the growth of harmful microorganisms in food, leading to spoilage and contamination.

Impact on public health and safety

Unintentional food adulteration can have serious consequences for public health and safety. It can cause foodborne illnesses, which can range from mild to severe, and in some cases, can be fatal. The impact of foodborne illnesses can be especially severe in vulnerable populations, such as children, elderly people, and individuals with weakened immune systems.

Measures to prevent unintentional food adulteration

To prevent unintentional food adulteration, various measures can be taken, including:

Good manufacturing practices: Implementing good manufacturing practices, such as maintaining proper hygiene and sanitation, can reduce the risk of unintentional contamination.

Quality control: Regular quality control measures, such as testing for contaminants, can help identify and prevent unintentional contamination.

Proper storage and transportation: Ensuring proper storage and transportation conditions for food products can help prevent unintentional contamination.

Regulatory oversight: Governments can establish and enforce regulations to ensure food safety and prevent unintentional contamination.

C. Examples of adulterants used in food

Adulterants are substances that are added to food intentionally or unintentionally to lower the quality of food. Some examples of adulterants used in food are:

Chemicals: Pesticides, fertilizers, artificial colors, preservatives, and sweeteners are some of the common chemicals that are added to food to improve its appearance and shelf life.

Biological agents: Pathogenic bacteria, viruses, and parasites are some examples of biological agents that can be present in food and cause illness.

Non-food materials: Sand, stones, sawdust, and other non-food materials are sometimes added to foods to increase weight or volume and therefore increase profits.

Contaminants: Contaminants can be either naturally occurring or man-made. Examples of natural contaminants include toxins produced by fungi or plants, while man-made contaminants include heavy metals, dioxins, and polychlorinated biphenyls (PCBs).

D. Health hazards of consuming adulterated food

Food adulteration can lead to various health hazards depending on the type of adulterant used and the level of contamination. Some of the health hazards associated with food adulteration include:

Food poisoning: Adulterants such as toxic chemicals, pesticides, and bacteria can cause food poisoning, which can lead to diarrhea, vomiting, nausea, and in severe cases, organ failure and death.

Allergic reactions: Adulterants such as undeclared allergens can cause allergic reactions in susceptible individuals, leading to symptoms such as swelling, hives, and difficulty breathing.

Chronic diseases: Long-term consumption of adulterated food can lead to chronic diseases such as cancer, heart disease, and liver and kidney damage.

Nutrient deficiencies: Adulteration can lead to a loss of essential nutrients in food, leading to nutrient deficiencies and related health problems.

Mental and neurological disorders: Certain adulterants such as heavy metals can accumulate in the body over time and lead to mental and neurological disorders such as dementia and Parkinson's disease.

D. Regulations and guidelines for preventing food adulteration

Regulations and guidelines are put in place to prevent food adulteration and ensure that consumers are protected from the health hazards associated with consuming adulterated food. The following are some of the regulations and guidelines aimed at preventing food adulteration:

Food Safety and Standards Act, 2006: This Act regulates the manufacture, distribution, and sale of food products in India. It lays down standards for food products and prescribes penalties for non-compliance.

Prevention of Food Adulteration Act, 1954: This Act regulates the prevention of food adulteration and lays down penalties for non-compliance. It defines adulteration and provides for the appointment of food inspectors to enforce the provisions of the Act.

Food Safety and Standards (Food Products Standards and Food Additives) Regulations, 2011: These regulations lay down the standards for various food products and food additives in India.

Bureau of Indian Standards (BIS): The BIS is responsible for laying down standards for various products, including food products, in India.

HACCP (Hazard Analysis and Critical Control Points) system: The HACCP system is a preventive approach to food safety that involves identifying potential hazards in the food production process and implementing measures to control them.

GMPs (Good Manufacturing Practices): GMPs are guidelines that outline the processes and procedures that food manufacturers must follow to ensure that their products are safe and of high quality.

Adulteration Detection Programs: Adulteration detection programs involve the use of various techniques and methods to detect adulterants in food products. These programs help to ensure that only safe and pure food products are sold to consumers.

IX. Regulations and Claims

A. Label Claims

Definition and purpose of label claims:

Label claims are statements made on the label of a food product that describe the nutritional content or health benefits of the product. These claims are intended to provide consumers with information about the product and help them make informed decisions about their food choices. Label claims can also be used as a marketing tool to promote a product's nutritional benefits or health advantages.

Types of label claims:

Nutrient content claims: These claims describe the amount of a nutrient in a product, such as "low fat," "high fiber," or "reduced sugar."

Health claims: These claims describe a relationship between a nutrient or ingredient in a product and its potential health benefits, such as "may reduce the risk of heart disease."

Structure/function claims: These claims describe the role of a nutrient or ingredient in maintaining normal body structure or function, such as "supports healthy immune function."

FDA regulations for label claims:

The FDA regulates label claims to ensure that they are truthful and not misleading. The regulations require that all claims be supported by scientific evidence and that they are not presented in a way that suggests the product can prevent or cure a disease.

Nutrient content claims must meet specific criteria, such as "low fat" must contain 3 grams or less of fat per serving. Health claims must be authorized by the FDA and supported by significant scientific agreement. Structure/function claims do not require FDA authorization, but they must be truthful and not misleading.

Food manufacturers are responsible for ensuring that their label claims comply with FDA regulations, and failure to do so can result in enforcement actions, including product seizure and recall.

B. Nutrient Content Claims

Definition and purpose of Nutrient Content Claims:

Nutrient content claims are the claims made on food labeling that describes the level of a particular nutrient in a food item. The purpose of nutrient content claims is to provide information to consumers about the nutrient content of a food item and to help them make healthier food choices. Nutrient content claims are used to highlight the positive nutritional aspects of a food item and can help consumers select foods that fit their dietary needs.

Examples of nutrient content claims:

"Low fat"

"Reduced sodium"

"High fiber"

"Cholesterol-free"

"Low calorie"

FDA regulations for nutrient content claims:

The FDA has established specific criteria that must be met in order for a food item to make a nutrient content claim. The criteria vary depending on the nutrient and the claim being made. For example, in order for a food item to be labeled as "low fat", it must contain 3 grams or less of fat per serving. The criteria for other nutrient content claims, such as "high fiber" or "reduced sodium", are also based on specific levels of the nutrient per serving.

The FDA also requires that the nutrient content claim be truthful and not misleading. This means that the claim must accurately reflect the nutrient content of the food item and not create a false impression about the health benefits of the food. In addition, the FDA may require that the food item meet certain standards of identity in order to make a nutrient content claim.

C. Health Claims

Health claims are statements on a food product that suggests a relationship between the consumption of that food and a reduced risk of a disease or health-related condition. The purpose of health claims is to provide consumers with information about the health benefits of a food product so they can make informed choices about what they eat.

Examples of health claims include:

- "Diets low in saturated fat and cholesterol and high in fruits, vegetables, and grain products that contain some types of dietary fiber, particularly soluble fiber, may reduce the risk of heart disease, a disease associated with many factors."
- "Calcium and vitamin D may reduce the risk of osteoporosis."
- "Low sodium intake may reduce the risk of high blood pressure, a disease associated with many factors."

The FDA regulates health claims on food products to ensure that they are truthful and not misleading. Before a health claim can be used on a food product, the FDA must review and authorize it based on scientific evidence. The FDA has established a process for reviewing health claims that includes the following:

- The claim must be based on a significant scientific agreement.
- The claim must be supported by the weight of the scientific evidence.
- The claim must be appropriately qualified to avoid misleading consumers.

If a food product bears a health claim that has not been authorized by the FDA or does not meet the FDA's criteria, the product is considered misbranded and is subject to regulatory action.

D. Dietary Supplements Claims

Introduction:

Dietary supplements are products taken orally that contain one or more dietary ingredients intended to supplement one's diet. They can include vitamins, minerals, herbs, amino acids, and other substances. Claims made on dietary supplements are regulated by the U.S. Food and Drug Administration (FDA) under the Dietary Supplement Health and Education Act (DSHEA) of 1994. The regulations for dietary supplements claims differ from those for food products.

Dietary Supplements Claims:

Dietary supplements claims refer to the statements made on the label of a dietary supplement about the effects of the product on the body. The FDA requires that all claims made on dietary supplements be truthful and not misleading. The three main types of dietary supplements claims are:

Health claims: These claims describe a relationship between a nutrient or ingredient in the supplement and a disease or health-related condition. For example, a health claim on a supplement containing calcium might state that calcium helps reduce the risk of osteoporosis.

Structure/function claims: These claims describe how a nutrient or ingredient in the supplement affects the structure or function of the body. For example, a structure/function claim on a supplement containing iron might state that iron helps transport oxygen in the body.

Nutrient content claims: These claims describe the amount of a nutrient or dietary ingredient in a supplement. For example, a nutrient content claim on a supplement containing vitamin C might state that it provides "100% of the recommended daily intake of vitamin C."

FDA Regulations for Dietary Supplements Claims:

Under DSHEA, the FDA regulates dietary supplements as a category of food, rather than as drugs. This means that manufacturers of dietary supplements are responsible for ensuring the safety and accuracy of their products' claims. The FDA has established regulations for dietary supplements claims, including the following:

Health claims: In order to make a health claim on a dietary supplement, the manufacturer must have scientific evidence to support the claim. The FDA must review the evidence and approve the claim before it can be used on the supplement label.

Structure/function claims: Structure/function claims do not require FDA approval before they can be used on a dietary supplement label. However, the manufacturer must have scientific evidence to support the claim and must include a disclaimer on the label that the FDA has not evaluated the claim.

Nutrient content claims: Nutrient content claims on dietary supplements are subject to the same regulations as nutrient content claims on food products. The manufacturer must ensure that the claim is truthful and not misleading, and must meet specific criteria established by the FDA for each nutrient.

X. Current Issues in Food Safety

A. Emerging foodborne illnesses:

Emerging foodborne illnesses refer to infectious diseases caused by microorganisms that were not previously known or have increased in incidence or geographic range. Some examples of recent emerging foodborne illnesses include E. coli O157:H7, Salmonella serotype Enteritidis, and Listeria monocytogenes.

The causes of emerging foodborne illnesses can vary, but some common contributing factors include changes in food production and distribution systems, global travel and trade, and changes in consumer behavior and preferences. For example, the increased demand for fresh produce and convenience foods has led to changes in production and distribution methods that may increase the risk of contamination.

Prevention and control strategies for emerging foodborne illnesses include improved surveillance and monitoring systems, increased research on the causes and prevention of these illnesses, and the implementation of food safety management systems such as HACCP. In addition, consumer education and awareness can play a critical role in preventing the spread of emerging foodborne illnesses.

B. Genetically modified foods:

Explanation of genetically modified foods:

Genetically modified foods, also known as genetically engineered foods, are produced from organisms whose genetic material has been modified in a way that does not occur naturally through traditional breeding methods. This modification is usually done by introducing genes from other organisms to produce desirable traits such as resistance to pests, herbicides, or disease.

Pros and cons of genetically modified foods:

Proponents of genetically modified foods argue that they have several benefits, such as increased crop yields, reduced use of pesticides and herbicides, and the potential to address global food insecurity by producing crops that are more resilient to environmental stressors. However, opponents of genetically modified foods raise concerns about their safety, the potential environmental impact of growing genetically modified crops, and the ethical implications of modifying the genetic makeup of organisms.

FDA regulations and guidelines for genetically modified foods:

The FDA regulates genetically modified foods under the Federal Food, Drug, and Cosmetic Act and ensures their safety before they are sold in the market. The FDA evaluates genetically modified foods on a case-by-case basis and requires manufacturers to provide data on the safety and nutritional content of the modified food. The FDA also requires that genetically modified foods be labeled as such if they differ significantly from their non-genetically modified counterparts.

Consumer perceptions and concerns about genetically modified foods:

Consumer perceptions and concerns about genetically modified foods vary widely. Some consumers see genetically modified foods as a potential solution to global food insecurity and support their development and use. Others have concerns about the potential health and environmental risks of genetically modified foods and prefer to avoid them. Labeling of genetically modified foods has become a contentious issue, with some consumers arguing for mandatory labeling to allow them to make informed purchasing decisions.

C. Organic foods:

Organic foods are those produced without the use of synthetic pesticides, fertilizers, or genetically modified organisms (GMOs). They are grown and processed using natural and sustainable farming methods that promote soil and water conservation and reduce pollution. Organic foods are becoming increasingly popular due to their perceived health benefits, environmental friendliness, and ethical considerations.

Benefits of organic foods include:

Reduced exposure to pesticides and chemicals: Organic farming practices minimize the use of synthetic pesticides, herbicides, and fertilizers, which can have harmful effects on human health and the environment.

Better nutrient content: Organic foods are often richer in nutrients like vitamins, minerals, and antioxidants than conventionally grown foods.

Environmental sustainability: Organic farming practices promote soil health, conserve water, and reduce pollution and greenhouse gas emissions.

Drawbacks of organic foods include:

Higher cost: Organic foods are often more expensive than conventionally grown foods due to the higher cost of production.

Limited availability: Organic foods may not be readily available in some areas, especially in rural or remote regions.

Shorter shelf life: Organic foods tend to spoil faster than conventionally grown foods due to the lack of preservatives.

The United States Department of Agriculture (USDA) regulates organic foods under the National Organic Program (NOP). The NOP has established strict standards for organic production and labeling, including requirements for organic certification, labeling, and verification. Products labeled as "100% organic" must contain only organically produced ingredients, while those labeled "organic" must contain at least 95% organic ingredients.

Consumer perceptions of organic foods vary widely. Some people view them as a healthier and more environmentally sustainable alternative to conventionally grown foods, while others believe that the benefits of organic foods are exaggerated and not worth the higher cost. Trends in organic food consumption have been steadily increasing in recent years, with organic food sales in the United States reaching over $50 billion in 2020.

D. Food labeling controversies:

Food labeling controversies refer to the debates and concerns surrounding the labeling practices used by food manufacturers and marketers. These labeling practices include claims related to the nutritional content of the food, the use of certain ingredients, and the production methods employed.

Examples of controversial food labeling practices include "natural," "organic," and "GMO-free" claims. The use of the term "natural" on food labels has been debated because it lacks a clear definition, and some companies have used it to market products containing artificial or synthetic ingredients. Similarly, the use of the term "organic" on food labels is regulated by the USDA, but there is still debate about the actual benefits of organic foods and the accuracy of organic labeling.

Another controversial labeling practice is the use of "GMO-free" claims. While genetically modified organisms (GMOs) have been deemed safe by regulatory agencies such as the FDA, some consumers have expressed concerns about the potential long-term health and environmental impacts of GMOs. The use of "GMO-free" claims has been criticized for being misleading or unnecessary, as GMOs have not been shown to pose any significant risks to human health.

The FDA regulates food labeling practices in the United States and provides guidelines for the use of certain claims on food packaging. For example, the FDA has specific rules for the use of health claims on food packaging, and it regulates the use of the term "organic" on food labels through the USDA's National Organic Program.

Consumer perspectives and advocacy play a significant role in food labeling controversies. Consumer demand for more transparency in food labeling has led to increased scrutiny of labeling practices and increased pressure on manufacturers to provide more accurate and informative labels. Consumer advocacy groups have also been instrumental in advocating for changes in food labeling regulations and practices.

VI

MCQs

Chapter 1. Functional Foods, Nutraceuticals, and Dietary Supplements: Sources and Health Benefits

1. Which of the following is a definition of nutraceuticals? A) Foods that have been genetically modified B) Foods that have been fortified with vitamins and minerals C) Foods that have health benefits beyond basic nutrition D) Foods that are only available with a prescription Correct answer: C) Foods that have health benefits beyond basic nutrition Explanation: Nutraceuticals are foods that have additional health benefits beyond basic nutrition.
2. Which of the following is a health problem that can be prevented or managed by nutraceuticals? A) Broken bones B) Cataracts C) Malaria D) Diabetes Correct answer: D) Diabetes Explanation: Nutraceuticals have been shown to have potential in preventing and

managing chronic diseases such as diabetes.

3. Which of the following is a marker compound in Spirulina? A) Beta-carotene B) Caffeine C) Iron D) Calcium Correct answer: A) Beta-carotene Explanation: Beta-carotene is a marker compound in Spirulina, which is a type of blue-green algae.
4. What is the medicinal use of ginseng as a nutraceutical? A) To treat hypertension B) To prevent tooth decay C) To cure arthritis D) To improve eyesight Correct answer: A) To treat hypertension Explanation: Ginseng is commonly used as a nutraceutical to treat hypertension.
5. Which of the following is a marker compound in broccoli? A) Vitamin C B) Resveratrol C) Sulforaphane D) Lycopene Correct answer: C) Sulforaphane Explanation: Sulforaphane is a marker compound in broccoli, which is known for its potential anti-cancer properties.
6. What is the health benefit of flaxseeds as a nutraceutical? A) Improving cognitive function B) Treating depression C) Lowering cholesterol D) Reducing inflammation Correct answer: C) Lowering cholesterol Explanation: Flaxseeds are commonly used as a nutraceutical for their potential to lower cholesterol levels.
7. Which of the following is a potential benefit of nutraceuticals? A) Improved cardiovascular health B) Reduced risk of injury from physical activity C) Increased likelihood of developing chronic diseases D) None of the above Answer: A) Improved cardiovascular health. Nutraceuticals have been shown to possess various biological activities such as antioxidant, anti-inflammatory, and anti-cancer properties, which make them attractive for disease prevention and management. They may also provide additional benefits

such as improved cognitive function, immune system function, and gastrointestinal health.

8. Which of the following is an example of a dietary supplement? A) Spirulina B) Broccoli C) Flaxseeds D) None of the above Answer: A) Spirulina. Dietary supplements are products that contain one or more dietary ingredients such as vitamins, minerals, herbs, amino acids, or other substances. Spirulina is a type of blue-green algae that is often consumed in supplement form for its high nutrient content.
9. Which of the following health problems may be prevented or managed through the use of nutraceuticals? A) Cardiovascular disease B) Type 2 diabetes C) Obesity D) All of the above Answer: D) All of the above. Nutraceuticals have been shown to possess various biological activities such as antioxidant, anti-inflammatory, and anti-cancer properties, which make them attractive for disease prevention and management. They may also provide additional benefits such as improved cognitive function, immune system function, and gastrointestinal health.
10. Which of the following is an example of a phytochemical that may be found in nutraceuticals? A) Sodium B) Lycopene C) Caffeine D) None of the above Answer: B) Lycopene. Phytochemicals are bioactive compounds found in plant-based foods and may provide health benefits when consumed. Lycopene is a carotenoid found in tomatoes and other red fruits and vegetables that is believed to have antioxidant properties.
11. Which of the following is an example of a prebiotic that may be found in nutraceuticals? A) Lactobacillus B) Fructo-oligosaccharides C) Resveratrol D) None of the

above Answer: B) Fructo-oligosaccharides. Prebiotics are a type of fiber that feed the beneficial bacteria in the gut, promoting digestive health. Fructo-oligosaccharides are a type of prebiotic commonly found in nutraceuticals.

12. Which of the following is an example of an endogenous antioxidant? A) Vitamin E B) Butylated hydroxyanisole (BHA) C) Glutathione D) None of the above Answer: C) Glutathione. Endogenous antioxidants are produced by the body and include enzymes such as superoxide dismutase, catalase, and glutathione peroxidase. Glutathione is a non-enzymatic antioxidant that plays a key role in protecting cells from oxidative damage.
13. Which of the following is NOT a potential health benefit of nutraceuticals? A) Improved cognitive function B) Improved immune system function C) Improved cardiovascular health D) Increased risk of chronic disease Answer: D) Increased risk of chronic disease. Nutraceuticals are believed to have potential benefits for preventing and managing chronic diseases.
14. Which of the following is a type of phytochemical found in plants that has potential health benefits as a nutraceutical? A) Amino acids B) Carbohydrates C) Polyphenols D) Saturated fats Answer: C) Polyphenols. Polyphenols are a class of phytochemicals found in plants that have antioxidant properties and potential health benefits.
15. Which of the following is an example of a prebiotic that can be classified as a nutraceutical? A) Lycopene B) Fructo-oligosaccharides C) Resveratrol D) Butylated hydroxytoluene Answer: B) Fructo-oligosaccharides. Prebiotics are types of fiber that promote the growth of beneficial bacteria in the gut, and fructo-oligosaccharides are an example of a prebiotic that can

be classified as a nutraceutical.

16. Which of the following is a potential health benefit of consuming nutraceuticals containing phytoestrogens? A) Improved cardiovascular health B) Reduced risk of cancer C) Improved bone health D) Reduced risk of infectious diseases Answer: C) Improved bone health. Phytoestrogens are compounds found in plants that can have estrogen-like effects in the body and may help to improve bone health.
17. Which of the following is a regulatory agency responsible for ensuring food safety in the United States? A) USDA B) EPA C) FDA D) CDC Answer: C) FDA. The FDA, or Food and Drug Administration, is responsible for ensuring the safety of food, drugs, and other products in the United States.
18. Which of the following is an example of a claim that can be made on a food label for a nutraceutical product? A) "This product has been proven to cure cancer." B) "This product is 100% natural." C) "This product will help you lose 10 pounds in one week." D) "This product contains vitamin C, which supports immune system health." Answer: D) "This product contains vitamin C, which supports immune system health." Nutrient content claims and health claims are allowed on food labels for nutraceutical products, but disease cure claims or weight loss claims may not be allowed without appropriate scientific evidence to support them.
19. Which of the following is a source of Spirulina? A) Ginger B) Soybean C) Broccoli D) Algae Answer: D) Algae. Spirulina is a type of blue-green algae.
20. Which of the following is a marker compound found in garlic? A) Resveratrol B) Allicin C) Lutein D) Catechins Answer: B) Allicin. Allicin is a sulfur-containing

compound found in garlic.

21. What is the potential health benefit of consuming ginseng as a nutraceutical? A) Improved brain function B) Reduced risk of heart disease C) Increased bone density D) Improved vision Answer: A) Improved brain function. Ginseng has been shown to have cognitive-enhancing effects.
22. Which of the following is a potential use of flaxseeds as a nutraceutical? A) Improved joint health B) Lowered blood sugar levels C) Increased muscle mass D) Improved lung function Answer: B) Lowered blood sugar levels. Flaxseeds are a good source of fiber and have been shown to improve glycemic control in people with type 2 diabetes.
23. Which of the following is a potential health benefit of consuming lycopene? A) Reduced risk of cancer B) Improved immune system function C) Reduced risk of osteoporosis D) Improved skin elasticity Answer: A) Reduced risk of cancer. Lycopene is a carotenoid that has been shown to have anti-cancer properties.
24. Which of the following is a potential use of probiotics as a nutraceutical? A) Lowering blood pressure B) Reducing inflammation C) Increasing muscle strength D) Improving lung function Answer: B) Reducing inflammation. Probiotics have been shown to have anti-inflammatory effects in the gut and other parts of the body.
25. Which of the following is a source of prebiotics? A. Spirulina B. Soybean C. Lactobacillus D. Fructo-oligosaccharides (FOS) Answer: D. Fructo-oligosaccharides (FOS) are a type of prebiotic that stimulate the growth of beneficial bacteria in the gut.

26. Which of the following phytochemicals is associated with red wine? A. Resveratrol B. Lycopene C. Flavonoids D. Catechins Answer: A. Resveratrol is a polyphenolic compound found in grapes and is associated with the health benefits of red wine.
27. Which of the following is an example of a dietary supplement? A. Broccoli B. Soybean C. Vitamin C D. Garlic Answer: C. Vitamin C is a dietary supplement that is commonly consumed to boost the immune system.
28. Which of the following health benefits is associated with consuming garlic? A. Improved cognitive function B. Prevention of cancer C. Regulation of blood sugar levels D. Improved cardiovascular health Answer: D. Garlic has been shown to improve cardiovascular health by reducing blood pressure and cholesterol levels.
29. Which of the following is an example of a carotenoid? A. Resveratrol B. Lutein C. Quercetin D. Curcumin Answer: B. Lutein is a carotenoid that is found in green leafy vegetables and is important for eye health.
30. Which of the following is a regulatory agency for food safety in the United States? A. FPO B. MPO C. AGMARK D. FDA Answer: D. The FDA (Food and Drug Administration) is a regulatory agency in the United States that is responsible for ensuring the safety of food and drugs.

Chapter 2. Phytochemicals as Nutraceuticals

1. Which of the following phytochemicals is known for its antioxidant properties? A) Xanthophylls B) Diallylsulfides C) Resveratrol D) Lactobacillus Answer: C.

Resveratrol is a polyphenolic compound found in plants and is known for its antioxidant properties.

2. Which of the following phytochemicals is found in broccoli and is known to have anticancer properties? A) Rutin B) Lycopene C) Resveratrol D) Sulforaphane Answer: D. Sulforaphane is a sulfide compound found in broccoli and is known to have anticancer properties.
3. Which of the following phytochemicals is commonly found in citrus fruits and has anti-inflammatory properties? A) Naringin B) Lutein C) Tocopherols D) Allyltrisulfide Answer: A. Naringin is a flavonoid compound found in citrus fruits and has been shown to have anti-inflammatory properties.
4. Which of the following phytochemicals is known for its cholesterol-lowering effects? A) Isoflavones B) Lignans C) β-Carotene D) Quercetin Answer: A. Isoflavones are a type of phytoestrogen found in soybeans and are known for their cholesterol-lowering effects.
5. Which of the following phytochemicals is a prebiotic and is commonly found in foods like onions and garlic? A) Fructo-oligosaccharides B) Diallylsulfides C) Xanthophylls D) Catechins Answer: A. Fructo-oligosaccharides are a type of prebiotic found in foods like onions and garlic and are known to promote the growth of beneficial gut bacteria.
6. Which of the following phytochemicals is a form of vitamin E and has antioxidant properties? A) Tocopherols B) Lycopene C) Daidzein D) Rutin Answer: A. Tocopherols are a form of vitamin E found in various foods and are known for their antioxidant properties.
7. Which of the following phytochemicals is known for its antioxidant properties? A) Lycopene B) Diallylsulfides C) Fructo oligosaccharides D) Isoflavones Answer: A)

Lycopene. Lycopene is a carotenoid that is known for its antioxidant properties.

8. Which phytochemical is found in soybean and is known for its estrogen-like properties? A) Lutein B) Resveratrol C) Quercetin D) Isoflavones Answer: D) Isoflavones. Isoflavones are a type of phytoestrogen found in soybeans and are known for their estrogen-like properties.
9. Which of the following phytochemicals is found in garlic and has been shown to have anti-inflammatory and anti-cancer properties? A) Diallylsulfides B) Rutin C) Lycopene D) Resveratrol Answer: A) Diallylsulfides. Diallylsulfides are a type of sulfur compound found in garlic and have been shown to have anti-inflammatory and anti-cancer properties.
10. Which phytochemical is found in red wine and has been associated with cardiovascular health benefits? A) Lutein B) Resveratrol C) Quercetin D) Tocopherols Answer: B) Resveratrol. Resveratrol is a polyphenolic compound found in red wine and has been associated with cardiovascular health benefits.
11. Which of the following phytochemicals is found in broccoli and is known for its cancer-fighting properties? A) Lycopene B) Diallylsulfides C) Quercetin D) Sulforaphane Answer: D) Sulforaphane. Sulforaphane is a sulfur-containing compound found in broccoli and is known for its cancer-fighting properties.
12. Which of the following phytochemicals is found in green tea and has been shown to have antioxidant properties? A) Anthocyanidins B) Catechins C) Flavones D) Lycopene Answer: B) Catechins. Catechins are a type of flavonoid found in green tea and have been shown to have antioxidant properties.

13. Which of the following phytochemicals is known for its anti-inflammatory properties? A) Lycopene B) Resveratrol C) Isoflavones D) Tocopherols Answer: B. Resveratrol has been shown to possess anti-inflammatory properties, particularly in reducing inflammation in the cardiovascular system.
14. Which phytochemical is commonly found in citrus fruits and has been linked to improved cardiovascular health? A) Quercetin B) Rutin C) Naringin D) Lutein Answer: C. Naringin is a flavonoid commonly found in citrus fruits such as grapefruit and has been linked to improved cardiovascular health due to its ability to lower blood pressure and cholesterol levels.
15. Which phytochemical is known for its anti-cancer properties and is commonly found in green tea? A) Catechins B) Lutein C) Xanthophylls D) Resveratrol Answer: A. Catechins are flavonoids commonly found in green tea and have been shown to possess anti-cancer properties due to their ability to inhibit tumor growth and reduce oxidative stress.
16. Which phytochemical is commonly found in soybeans and is known for its estrogen-like effects? A) Diallylsulfides B) Lignans C) Allyltrisulfide D) Naringin Answer: B. Lignans are phytoestrogens commonly found in soybeans and have been shown to have estrogen-like effects, which may provide health benefits for women during menopause.
17. Which phytochemical is commonly found in spinach and has been linked to improved eye health? A) Lycopene B) Lutein C) Xanthophylls D) Quercetin Answer: B. Lutein is a xanthophyll commonly found in spinach and other leafy greens, and has been linked to improved eye health due to its ability to protect against oxidative

damage in the eyes.

18. Which phytochemical is a type of carotenoid commonly found in tomatoes and has been linked to reduced risk of prostate cancer? A) Lycopene B) Beta-carotene C) Lutein D) Quercetin Answer: A. Lycopene is a type of carotenoid commonly found in tomatoes and has been linked to reduced risk of prostate cancer due to its antioxidant properties.
19. Which of the following is a polyphenolic compound? A) Lycopene B) Quercetin C) Xanthophylls D) Diallylsulfides Answer: B) Quercetin. Explanation: Quercetin is a type of flavonoid and a polyphenolic compound found in various plant foods, such as onions, apples, and berries.
20. Which of the following is a source of prebiotics? A) Broccoli B) Soybean C) Fructo oligosaccharides D) Tocopherols Answer: C) Fructo oligosaccharides. Explanation: Fructo oligosaccharides are a type of prebiotic found in various plant foods, such as chicory root, asparagus, and bananas.
21. Which of the following compounds is commonly found in carrots and has antioxidant properties? A) Lycopene B) Quercetin C) β-carotene D) Diallylsulfides Answer: C) β-carotene. Explanation: β-carotene is a carotenoid and a precursor of vitamin A found in various plant foods, such as carrots, sweet potatoes, and spinach. It has antioxidant properties and is beneficial for eye health.
22. Which of the following compounds is a type of phytoestrogen? A) Allyltrisulfide B) Resveratrol C) Naringin D) Isoflavones Answer: D) Isoflavones. Explanation: Isoflavones are a type of phytoestrogen found in soybean and other legumes. They have been shown to have estrogen-like effects and may have health

benefits for women.

23. Which of the following compounds is commonly found in green tea and has anti-cancer properties? A) Lycopene B) Quercetin C) Catechins D) Diallylsulfides Answer: C) Catechins. Explanation: Catechins are a type of flavonoid found in green tea and have been shown to have anti-cancer properties.
24. Which of the following compounds is a type of tocopherol and has antioxidant properties? A) β-carotene B) Lycopene C) Tocotrienols D) Diallylsulfides Answer: C) Tocotrienols. Explanation: Tocotrienols are a type of tocopherol found in various plant foods, such as palm oil and rice bran, and have antioxidant properties.
25. Which of the following phytochemicals is known for its anti-inflammatory properties? A) Lycopene B) Resveratrol C) Quercetin D) Fructo oligosaccharides Answer: C) Quercetin. Quercetin is a flavonoid that has been shown to have anti-inflammatory properties.
26. Which of the following phytochemicals is found in broccoli and may have cancer-preventive properties? A) Diallylsulfides B) Xanthophylls C) Resveratrol D) Sulforaphane Answer: D) Sulforaphane. Sulforaphane is a compound found in broccoli and other cruciferous vegetables that has been shown to have cancer-preventive properties.
27. Which of the following phytochemicals is a type of carotenoid? A) Quercetin B) Resveratrol C) Lycopene D) Fructo oligosaccharides Answer: C) Lycopene. Lycopene is a carotenoid that is found in tomatoes, watermelon, and other red or pink fruits and vegetables.
28. Which of the following phytochemicals is a type of polyphenol? A) Rutin B) Lactobacillus C) Daidzein D) α-Tocopherol Answer: A) Rutin. Rutin is a type of

polyphenol that is found in many fruits and vegetables, including citrus fruits and buckwheat.

29. Which of the following phytochemicals is known for its prebiotic properties? A) Quercetin B) Diallylsulfides C) Fructo oligosaccharides D) Lignans Answer: C) Fructo oligosaccharides. Fructo oligosaccharides are a type of prebiotic that are found in many fruits and vegetables, including bananas and onions.
30. Which of the following phytochemicals is known for its antioxidant properties? A) Soybean B) Ginseng C) Tocopherols D) Garlic Answer: C) Tocopherols. Tocopherols, also known as vitamin E, are a group of antioxidants that are found in many nuts, seeds, and vegetable oils.

Chapter 3. Introduction to Free radicals and its Measurement

1. Which of the following is NOT a damaging reaction of free radicals? A) Oxidation of lipids B) Oxidation of proteins C) Oxidation of carbohydrates D) Hydrolysis of nucleic acids Answer: D. Hydrolysis of nucleic acids is not a damaging reaction of free radicals.
2. Which of the following is a measurement of free radicals? A) ATP production B) Lipid peroxidation products C) Protein synthesis D) Carbohydrate metabolism Answer: B. Lipid peroxidation products are a measurement of free radicals.
3. Which of the following is a reactive oxygen species? A) Hydrogen peroxide B) Carbon dioxide C) Nitrogen gas D) Oxygen gas Answer: A. Hydrogen peroxide is a reactive

oxygen species.

4. What is the production site of free radicals in cells? A) Mitochondria B) Golgi apparatus C) Endoplasmic reticulum D) Nucleus Answer: A. Mitochondria is the production site of free radicals in cells.
5. Which of the following is a lipid peroxidation product? A) Glucose B) Acetyl-CoA C) Malondialdehyde D) Glycerol Answer: C. Malondialdehyde is a lipid peroxidation product.
6. Which of the following is NOT a damaging effect of free radicals on cells? A) DNA damage B) Inflammation C) Cell proliferation D) Protein denaturation Answer: C. Free radicals do not damage cells by inhibiting cell proliferation.
7. Which of the following is an example of a reactive oxygen species? A) Hydrogen peroxide B) Water C) Carbon dioxide D) Nitrogen Answer: A) Hydrogen peroxide. Reactive oxygen species include hydrogen peroxide, superoxide, and hydroxyl radicals, among others.
8. Free radicals can damage which of the following biomolecules? A) Lipids B) Proteins C) Carbohydrates D) All of the above Answer: D) All of the above. Free radicals can react with and damage lipids, proteins, carbohydrates, and nucleic acids.
9. Malondialdehyde is a byproduct of: A) Lipid peroxidation B) Protein oxidation C) Carbohydrate oxidation D) Nucleic acid oxidation Answer: A) Lipid peroxidation. Malondialdehyde is a commonly used marker for lipid peroxidation, which is a damaging reaction of free radicals on lipids.
10. What is the main function of antioxidant enzymes like superoxide dismutase and catalase? A) To produce free

radicals B) To neutralize free radicals C) To increase free radical production D) To stimulate inflammation Answer: B) To neutralize free radicals. Antioxidant enzymes work to neutralize free radicals and prevent their damaging reactions.

11. Which of the following is an exogenous antioxidant? A) Glutathione B) Melatonin C) Vitamin E D) Superoxide dismutase Answer: C) Vitamin E. Exogenous antioxidants are those that come from outside the body, such as through diet or supplements, and include vitamins C and E, as well as flavonoids.
12. The free radical theory of aging proposes that aging is caused by: A) Genetic mutations B) Accumulation of free radical damage C) Exposure to toxins D) A lack of antioxidants Answer: B) Accumulation of free radical damage. The free radical theory of aging suggests that the accumulation of free radical damage over time contributes to the aging process.
13. Which of the following is a damaging reaction of free radicals on proteins? A. Protein denaturation B. Protein synthesis C. Protein phosphorylation D. Protein glycosylation Answer: A. Protein denaturation. Free radicals can cause oxidative damage to proteins, leading to their denaturation and loss of function.
14. What is the main product used to measure lipid peroxidation? A. Malondialdehyde (MDA) B. Superoxide dismutase (SOD) C. Catalase D. Glutathione peroxidase (GPx) Answer: A. Malondialdehyde (MDA). MDA is one of the end products of lipid peroxidation and is commonly used as a marker of oxidative stress.
15. Which of the following is a reactive oxygen species (ROS)? A. Nitric oxide (NO) B. Carbon dioxide (CO2) C. Hydrogen peroxide (H2O2) D. Methane (CH4) Answer: C.

Hydrogen peroxide (H_2O_2). H_2O_2 is a type of ROS that can cause oxidative damage to cells and tissues.

16. What is the main source of free radicals in cells? A. Mitochondria B. Nucleus C. Ribosomes D. Cell membrane Answer: A. Mitochondria. Mitochondria are the main source of free radicals in cells due to their role in cellular respiration and energy production.
17. What is the primary damaging effect of free radicals on nucleic acids? A. DNA replication B. RNA transcription C. DNA damage D. RNA degradation Answer: C. DNA damage. Free radicals can cause oxidative damage to DNA, leading to mutations and other DNA damage.
18. Which of the following is an enzyme that helps to reduce oxidative stress in cells? A. Superoxide dismutase (SOD) B. Hydrogen peroxide (H_2O_2) C. Malondialdehyde (MDA) D. Nitric oxide (NO) Answer: A. Superoxide dismutase (SOD). SOD is an enzyme that helps to convert superoxide radicals into less harmful substances, reducing oxidative stress in cells.
19. Which of the following is not a damaging reaction of free radicals? A. Oxidation of lipids B. Glycation of proteins C. Cross-linking of nucleic acids D. Disruption of carbohydrates Answer: D. Disruption of carbohydrates. Free radicals can cause oxidative damage to lipids, proteins, and nucleic acids, but not carbohydrates.
20. Which of the following is a lipid peroxidation product? A. Superoxide anion B. Hydrogen peroxide C. Malondialdehyde D. Nitric oxide Answer: C. Malondialdehyde. It is a byproduct of the oxidation of polyunsaturated fatty acids in cell membranes.
21. What is the main type of reactive oxygen species? A. Hydrogen peroxide B. Superoxide anion C. Hydroxyl

radical D. Peroxynitrite Answer: C. Hydroxyl radical. It is the most reactive and damaging ROS due to its ability to react with almost any molecule in cells.

22. How can lipid hydroperoxide be measured? A. Western blotting B. ELISA C. Spectrophotometry D. Flow cytometry Answer: C. Spectrophotometry. It is a common method to measure lipid hydroperoxide levels, which is a marker of oxidative stress in cells.
23. Which of the following is a non-damaging reaction of free radicals? A. Oxidation of DNA B. Cross-linking of proteins C. Activation of antioxidant enzymes D. Formation of reactive nitrogen species Answer: C. Activation of antioxidant enzymes. Antioxidant enzymes, such as superoxide dismutase and catalase, are activated by free radicals and help neutralize their damaging effects.
24. What is the source of free radicals in cells? A. Mitochondria B. Nucleus C. Endoplasmic reticulum D. Ribosomes Answer: A. Mitochondria. They are the primary source of free radicals in cells due to their role in energy production and the generation of ROS as a byproduct.

Chapter 4. Free Radicals, Antioxidants, and Disease: Understanding the Role of Oxidative Stress in Health and Aging

1. Which of the following is an example of a nonenzymatic antioxidant? A) Superoxide dismutase B) Glutathione peroxidase C) Vitamin C D) Catalase Answer: C) Vitamin C. Nonenzymatic antioxidants are those that are not

produced by the body and must be obtained through diet or supplements. Vitamin C is an important water-soluble antioxidant that can scavenge free radicals and regenerate other antioxidants.

2. Which disorder is NOT associated with free radicals? A) Atherosclerosis B) Cancer C) Alzheimer's disease D) None of the above Answer: D) None of the above. Free radicals are involved in many disorders, including those listed in the options. Alzheimer's disease has been linked to oxidative stress and free radical damage in the brain.
3. What is the role of superoxide dismutase in antioxidant defense? A) It converts superoxide radicals to hydrogen peroxide. B) It breaks down hydrogen peroxide into water and oxygen. C) It scavenges hydroxyl radicals. D) It regenerates vitamin E. Answer: A) It converts superoxide radicals to hydrogen peroxide. Superoxide dismutase is an important antioxidant enzyme that converts superoxide radicals to hydrogen peroxide, which can then be further broken down by other enzymes.
4. Which synthetic antioxidant is commonly used in food preservation? A) Superoxide dismutase B) α-Lipoic acid C) Butylatedhydroxy Toluene D) Glutathione peroxidase Answer: C) Butylatedhydroxy Toluene. Synthetic antioxidants are often added to foods to prevent oxidation and spoilage. Butylatedhydroxy Toluene (BHT) is one such antioxidant that is commonly used in food preservation.
5. Which of the following is NOT a disorder that can be caused by free radicals? A) Diabetes mellitus B) Inflammation C) Genetic mutations D) Atherosclerosis Answer: C) Genetic mutations. While free radicals can damage DNA and contribute to mutations, it is not a disorder in and of itself.

6. What is the function of glutathione peroxidase in antioxidant defense? A) It converts superoxide radicals to hydrogen peroxide. B) It breaks down hydrogen peroxide into water and oxygen. C) It scavenges hydroxyl radicals. D) It reduces lipid peroxides to their corresponding alcohols. Answer: D) It reduces lipid peroxides to their corresponding alcohols. Glutathione peroxidase is an important antioxidant enzyme that reduces lipid peroxides to their corresponding alcohols, thus preventing lipid peroxidation and subsequent damage to cell membranes.
7. Which of the following is an example of an endogenous enzymatic antioxidant? A) Vitamin C B) Butylated hydroxytoluene C) Superoxide dismutase D) Resveratrol Answer: C) Superoxide dismutase is an endogenous enzymatic antioxidant that converts superoxide radicals into hydrogen peroxide, which is further metabolized by other enzymes.
8. Which of the following diseases is associated with increased production of free radicals? A) Alzheimer's disease B) Sickle cell anemia C) Hypothyroidism D) Osteoporosis Answer: A) Alzheimer's disease is associated with increased production of free radicals, which contribute to the neuronal damage in the brain.
9. Which of the following antioxidants is a fat-soluble vitamin? A) Vitamin C B) Glutathione C) Vitamin E D) Melatonin Answer: C) Vitamin E is a fat-soluble vitamin that protects cell membranes from oxidative damage by scavenging lipid peroxyl radicals.
10. Which of the following is an example of a non-enzymatic antioxidant? A) Superoxide dismutase B) Catalase C) Vitamin C D) Glutathione peroxidase Answer: C) Vitamin C is a non-enzymatic antioxidant

that can donate electrons to neutralize free radicals.

11. Which of the following conditions is associated with oxidative stress? A) Hypertension B) Hypotension C) Hypoglycemia D) Hyperthyroidism Answer: A) Hypertension is associated with oxidative stress, which contributes to the development of cardiovascular disease.
12. Which of the following is a synthetic antioxidant commonly used in food preservation? A) Vitamin E B) Melatonin C) Butylated hydroxytoluene D) Glutathione Answer: C) Butylated hydroxytoluene is a synthetic antioxidant commonly used in food preservation to prevent the oxidation of fats and oils.
13. Which of the following is an example of an endogenous enzymatic antioxidant? A) Vitamin C B) Vitamin E C) Superoxide dismutase D) Butylatedhydroxy Toluene Answer: C) Superoxide dismutase. Explanation: Superoxide dismutase is an example of an endogenous enzymatic antioxidant that catalyzes the conversion of superoxide radicals to less harmful molecules.
14. Which of the following is an example of a synthetic antioxidant? A) Glutathione B) Vitamin C C) Butylatedhydroxy Toluene D) Alpha-lipoic acid Answer: C) Butylatedhydroxy Toluene. Explanation: Butylatedhydroxy Toluene is a synthetic antioxidant commonly used as a food preservative to prevent lipid oxidation.
15. Free radicals are known to play a role in which of the following diseases? A) Arthritis B) Osteoporosis C) Alzheimer's disease D) All of the above Answer: C) Alzheimer's disease. Explanation: Free radicals are believed to contribute to the development and progression of many diseases, including Alzheimer's

disease, through oxidative damage to cells.

16. Which of the following is a non-enzymatic antioxidant? A) Catalase B) Superoxide dismutase C) Vitamin C D) Glutathione peroxidase Answer: C) Vitamin C. Explanation: Vitamin C is a non-enzymatic antioxidant that can donate electrons to neutralize free radicals and prevent oxidative damage.
17. Free radicals are produced during which of the following processes? A) Cellular respiration B) Photosynthesis C) Both A and B D) None of the above Answer: A) Cellular respiration. Explanation: Free radicals are produced during the normal metabolic processes of cells, such as cellular respiration, as well as through exposure to environmental toxins.
18. Which of the following is a potential health benefit of antioxidants? A) Reducing the risk of chronic diseases B) Enhancing athletic performance C) Improving cognitive function D) All of the above Answer: A) Reducing the risk of chronic diseases. Explanation: Antioxidants are believed to reduce the risk of chronic diseases by neutralizing free radicals and preventing oxidative damage to cells. While they may have other potential health benefits, such as enhancing athletic performance and improving cognitive function, more research is needed in these areas.
19. Which of the following is NOT an example of a disorder associated with free radicals? A) Diabetes mellitus B) Atherosclerosis C) Parkinson's disease D) None of the above Answer: D) None of the above. All of the disorders listed are associated with free radicals.
20. What is the role of antioxidants in the body? A) To promote the production of free radicals B) To neutralize free radicals and prevent oxidative damage C) To

enhance the damaging effects of free radicals D) None of the above Answer: B) To neutralize free radicals and prevent oxidative damage.

21. Which of the following is an example of an endogenous antioxidant? A) Vitamin C B) Vitamin E C) Glutathione peroxidase D) Butylatedhydroxy Toluene Answer: C) Glutathione peroxidase.
22. What is the function of superoxide dismutase? A) To neutralize superoxide radicals B) To neutralize hydroxyl radicals C) To neutralize peroxynitrite D) To promote the production of free radicals Answer: A) To neutralize superoxide radicals.
23. Which of the following is an example of a synthetic antioxidant? A) Glutathione peroxidase B) Butylatedhydroxy Toluene C) Superoxide dismutase D) None of the above Answer: B) Butylatedhydroxy Toluene.
24. Which of the following is an example of a non-enzymatic antioxidant? A) Superoxide dismutase B) Catalase C) Vitamin C D) Glutathione peroxidase Answer: C) Vitamin C.
25. Which of the following disorders is NOT associated with free radical damage? A) Diabetes mellitus B) Cancer C) Arthritis D) Atherosclerosis Answer: C) Arthritis. Explanation: Free radicals have been implicated in the pathogenesis of diabetes, cancer, atherosclerosis, and other disorders, but not arthritis.
26. Ischemic reperfusion injury is caused by: A) Inadequate blood flow to a tissue B) A sudden increase in blood pressure C) A sudden decrease in blood pressure D) Restoration of blood flow after a period of ischemia Answer: D) Restoration of blood flow after a period of ischemia. Explanation: Ischemic reperfusion injury occurs when blood flow is restored to a tissue after a

period of ischemia, leading to the generation of free radicals and other damaging molecules.

27. Which of the following is NOT an endogenous antioxidant? A) Glutathione peroxidase B) Superoxide dismutase C) Vitamin C D) Butylatedhydroxy Anisole Answer: D) Butylatedhydroxy Anisole. Explanation: Butylatedhydroxy Anisole is a synthetic antioxidant, while the others listed are all endogenous antioxidants.
28. Which of the following vitamins is a fat-soluble antioxidant? A) Vitamin C B) Vitamin E C) Vitamin D D) Vitamin B12 Answer: B) Vitamin E. Explanation: Vitamin E is a fat-soluble vitamin that acts as an antioxidant in cell membranes.
29. The free radical theory of aging suggests that aging is caused by: A) Accumulation of damage from free radicals over time B) A decrease in cellular metabolism C) A decrease in hormone production D) A decrease in protein synthesis Answer: A) Accumulation of damage from free radicals over time. Explanation: The free radical theory of aging suggests that aging is caused by the cumulative damage from free radicals that occurs over time.
30. Which of the following is an example of a nonenzymatic antioxidant defense? A) Superoxide dismutase B) Catalase C) Glutathione peroxidase D) Vitamin E Answer: D) Vitamin E. Explanation: Vitamin E is an example of a nonenzymatic antioxidant defense, while the others listed are all enzymatic antioxidants.
31. Which of the following disorders is NOT associated with free radicals? A) Diabetes mellitus B) Atherosclerosis C) Alzheimer's disease D) Osteoporosis Answer: D) Osteoporosis. Explanation: Although free radicals can be involved in a wide range of disorders, there is no direct

evidence linking them to osteoporosis.

32. Which of the following enzymes is an endogenous antioxidant? A) Superoxide dismutase B) Butylatedhydroxy Toluene C) Glutathione peroxidase D) Ascorbic acid Answer: A) Superoxide dismutase. Explanation: Superoxide dismutase is an enzyme that catalyzes the conversion of superoxide radicals to hydrogen peroxide, which can then be broken down further by other antioxidant enzymes.
33. Which of the following is a synthetic antioxidant? A) Vitamin E B) Glutathione C) Butylatedhydroxy Toluene D) Superoxide dismutase Answer: C) Butylatedhydroxy Toluene. Explanation: Butylatedhydroxy Toluene is a synthetic antioxidant that is commonly added to foods and personal care products to prevent oxidative damage.
34. Which of the following is NOT an enzymatic antioxidant? A) Superoxide dismutase B) Catalase C) Glutathione peroxidase D) Vitamin E Answer: D) Vitamin E. Explanation: Vitamin E is a non-enzymatic antioxidant that acts as a free radical scavenger in cell membranes.
35. Which of the following is a free radical theory of aging? A) Telomere shortening B) Wear and tear theory C) Hormonal theory D) Oxidative stress theory Answer: D) Oxidative stress theory. Explanation: The oxidative stress theory of aging proposes that the accumulation of oxidative damage caused by free radicals over time contributes to the aging process.
36. Which of the following is NOT a disorder that can be caused by free radicals? A) Cardiovascular disease B) Cancer C) Alzheimer's disease D) Arthritis Answer: D) Arthritis. Explanation: While inflammation and oxidative stress can contribute to the development of

arthritis, there is no direct evidence linking free radicals to this disorder.

37. Which of the following antioxidants is considered to be a universal antioxidant due to its ability to regenerate other antioxidants in the body? A) Vitamin E B) Vitamin C C) Glutathione D) Melatonin Answer: C) Glutathione. Explanation: Glutathione is a tripeptide composed of three amino acids and is involved in numerous physiological processes. It can also regenerate other antioxidants, making it a "universal antioxidant."
38. Which of the following conditions is not associated with increased production of free radicals? A) Diabetes mellitus B) Cancer C) Rheumatoid arthritis D) Hypertension Answer: D) Hypertension. Explanation: Although hypertension can have detrimental effects on health, it is not directly associated with increased production of free radicals.
39. Which of the following antioxidants can be found in green tea? A) Resveratrol B) Lycopene C) Epigallocatechin gallate (EGCG) D) Quercetin Answer: C) Epigallocatechin gallate (EGCG). Explanation: Green tea contains a variety of polyphenols, including EGCG, which has been shown to have antioxidant and anti-inflammatory effects.
40. Which of the following synthetic antioxidants is commonly used as a preservative in food and cosmetics? A) Butylatedhydroxytoluene (BHT) B) Melatonin C) α-Lipoic acid D) Glutathione Answer: A) Butylatedhydroxytoluene (BHT). Explanation: BHT is a commonly used synthetic antioxidant that helps to prevent the oxidation of fats and oils in food and cosmetics.

41. Which of the following is an enzymatic antioxidant? A) Vitamin E B) Superoxide dismutase C) Melatonin D) Butylatedhydroxytoluene (BHT) Answer: B) Superoxide dismutase. Explanation: Superoxide dismutase is an enzymatic antioxidant that helps to neutralize superoxide radicals.
42. Which of the following is not a health condition associated with increased production of free radicals? A) Atherosclerosis B) Alzheimer's disease C) Parkinson's disease D) Hypothyroidism Answer: D) Hypothyroidism. Explanation: While hypothyroidism can affect various aspects of health, it is not directly associated with increased production of free radicals.

Chapter 5. Food Laws, Regulations, and Claims: Ensuring Safety and Accuracy in the Food Industry

1. Which of the following is not a food regulatory agency in India? A) FDA B) FPO C) MPO D) EPA Correct answer: D) EPA. Explanation: The Food and Drug Administration (FDA), Food Safety and Standards Authority of India (FSSAI), Fruit Products Order (FPO), and Meat Products Order (MPO) are some of the food regulatory agencies in India. The Environmental Protection Agency (EPA) is not a food regulatory agency.
2. HACCP is a food safety management system that stands for: A) Hazard Analysis and Critical Control Points B) Hazardous Allergens and Critical Control Points C) Hazardous Analysis and Critical Condition Points D) Hazardous Allergens and Critical Condition Points

Correct answer: A) Hazard Analysis and Critical Control Points Explanation: HACCP is a food safety management system that focuses on identifying and controlling potential hazards in food production and processing. It stands for Hazard Analysis and Critical Control Points.

3. GMPs are: A) Good Manufacturing Processes B) Good Manufacturing Practices C) Good Management Processes D) Good Management Practices Correct answer: B) Good Manufacturing Practices Explanation: GMPs stand for Good Manufacturing Practices. They are a set of guidelines that ensure that food products are consistently produced and controlled to meet quality standards.
4. Adulteration of food refers to: A) Adding harmful substances to food B) Adding excess nutrients to food C) Adding flavor enhancers to food D) Adding preservatives to food Correct answer: A) Adding harmful substances to food Explanation: Adulteration of food refers to the addition of harmful substances to food, such as chemicals, dyes, or other substances that can cause health problems.
5. Nutrient content claims on food labels refer to: A) Claims about the safety of the food product B) Claims about the taste of the food product C) Claims about the nutrient content of the food product D) Claims about the price of the food product Correct answer: C) Claims about the nutrient content of the food product Explanation: Nutrient content claims on food labels refer to claims about the nutrient content of the food product, such as "low fat," "high fiber," or "good source of vitamin C."
6. Health claims on food labels refer to: A) Claims about the safety of the food product B) Claims about the taste of

the food product C) Claims about the nutrient content of the food product D) Claims about the relationship between the food product and a specific health condition Correct answer: D) Claims about the relationship between the food product and a specific health condition Explanation: Health claims on food labels refer to claims about the relationship between the food product and a specific health condition, such as "may reduce the risk of heart disease." These claims must be supported by scientific evidence and approved by the regulatory agency.

7. What does HACCP stand for? A) Hazard Analysis and Critical Control Points B) Health and Consumer Care Protection C) High Accuracy Calibration and Control Procedure D) Hazardous Air Control and Containment Program Answer: A) Hazard Analysis and Critical Control Points. HACCP is a food safety management system that identifies potential hazards in the food production process and establishes critical control points to prevent or eliminate them.
8. What is the purpose of the FDA? A) To regulate food safety in the United States B) To promote the interests of food manufacturers C) To enforce international food standards D) To monitor the nutritional content of food products Answer: A) To regulate food safety in the United States. The FDA (Food and Drug Administration) is responsible for ensuring the safety, efficacy, and security of human and veterinary drugs, biological products, medical devices, food supply, cosmetics, and products that emit radiation.
9. What is adulteration of food? A) The addition of harmful substances to food B) The removal of essential nutrients from food C) The use of deceptive packaging or labeling

D) The contamination of food by bacteria or viruses Answer: A) The addition of harmful substances to food. Adulteration of food refers to the intentional addition of harmful or cheaper substances to food products in order to increase the quantity or improve their appearance.

10. What is the purpose of GMPs in food production? A) To ensure the quality and safety of food products B) To increase the efficiency of food production C) To reduce the cost of food production D) To promote international trade of food products Answer: A) To ensure the quality and safety of food products. Good Manufacturing Practices (GMPs) are a set of guidelines for food production that ensure the safety, quality, and consistency of food products.
11. What is AGMARK? A) A certification mark used on agricultural products in India B) A government agency responsible for food safety in the United States C) A standard for food safety in Europe D) A quality assurance system for food production in Australia Answer: A) A certification mark used on agricultural products in India. AGMARK is a certification mark used on agricultural products in India that indicates that the product meets certain quality standards set by the government.
12. What is the main purpose of HACCP in the food industry? A) To ensure compliance with food labeling laws B) To prevent food contamination and ensure food safety C) To promote the sale of high-quality food products D) To reduce the cost of food production Answer: B) To prevent food contamination and ensure food safety. HACCP stands for Hazard Analysis and Critical Control Points, and it is a systematic approach to preventing food contamination and ensuring food

safety.

13. Which of the following is a common adulterant in milk? A) Starch B) Water C) Sand D) All of the above Answer: B) Water. Adulteration of milk with water is a common practice that can lead to economic fraud and pose a health risk to consumers.
14. Which regulatory body is responsible for ensuring the safety and efficacy of dietary supplements in the United States? A) FDA B) USDA C) FTC D) EPA Answer: A) FDA. The FDA is responsible for regulating the safety and efficacy of dietary supplements in the United States.
15. What is the purpose of food labeling laws? A) To promote the sale of food products B) To provide consumers with accurate information about the contents of food products C) To reduce the cost of food production D) To ensure compliance with HACCP regulations
16. Answer: B) To provide consumers with accurate information about the contents of food products. Food labeling laws require food manufacturers to provide accurate and comprehensive information about the ingredients and nutritional content of their products.
17. Which of the following is a requirement of GMPs in the food industry? A) Regular testing of finished products for contamination B) Proper labeling of food products C) Use of approved food additives and ingredients D) All of the above
18. Answer: D) All of the above. Good Manufacturing Practices (GMPs) require food manufacturers to adhere to strict standards for cleanliness, safety, and quality, including regular testing for contamination, proper labeling of food products, and use of approved food additives and ingredients.

9 798890 025128

Printed by Libri Plureos GmbH in Hamburg,
Germany